This book is dedicated to my husband, Lou, and my son, Alexander, with love and gratitude.

And to mothers everywhere, I honor you and the incredibly valuable contributions you make.

For A Very Special Friend! All My Love and God Bless! Sharon

I was inspired to write this book after reading Anne Wilson Schaef's *Meditations for Women Who Do Too Much*. The 365 meditations and provocative quotations sustained me through many a day's hectic schedule. But after the birth of my son, I wanted a book of meditations more specifically designed for my life as a new mother. I had so many questions during that first year—about the profound changes I was going through, about my new relationship to my husband, and about my roller-coaster emotions from exhilaration to exhaustion, from bliss to anger. I needed a wise friend who understood; I wanted other mothers to validate my experience and to assure me that I was not alone in my feelings.

Thus, *Meditations For New Mothers* tries to address the full range of emotions, conflicts, wonders, resentments, and plain old day-to-day issues that arise in early motherhood, especially among first-timers. The meditations do not tell you what to do or what kind of mother you should be. They are not answers. They are intended to get you thinking, to give you perspective on what's truly important, to even raise a smile. Most importantly, these meditations validate and celebrate our experiences as mothers since so much of what we do is hidden and cannot be measured.

MEDITATIONS
—*for*—
NEW MOTHERS

by
Beth Wilson Saavedra

❧

Illustrations
by
Lonni Sue Johnson

WORKMAN PUBLISHING, NEW YORK

Cover illustration by Lonni Sue Johnson

Library of Congress Cataloging-in-Publication Data

Saavedra, Beth Wilson.
Meditations for new mothers / by Beth Wilson Saavedra.
p. cm.
Includes biobliographical references and index.
ISBN 1-56305-181-8 (pbk.)
1. Mothers—Prayer-books and devotions—English. 2.
Devotional calendars. I. Title.
BL625.68.S33 1992
306.874′3—dc20   91-50961
                                                          CIP

Workman books are available at special discounts
when purchased in bulk for premiums and sales promotions
as well as for fund-raising or educational use. Special
editions can also be created to specification. For details,
contact the Special Sales Director at the address below.

Workman Publishing Company, Inc.
708 Broadway
New York, NY 10003

Manufactured in the United States of America

First printing June 1992

10   9   8   7   6   5   4   3   2   1

Since I know new mothers have little leisure time, I tried to make each meditation brief—a one page thought to read and reflect on throughout the day. Of course, this book is not just for recent or first-time moms. It is for all women who are raising children.

This book could not have been written without the loving support and encouragement of a number of people. I especially want to thank the following:

My parents, Anne and Paul, for your love, laughter and lessons.

Alexander's grandparents, for giving him your love and the special gift of your time.

Those friends who encouraged me to write this book: Lee Durland, Jillian Klarl, Todd Nelson, Ginger Hinchman, Betsy Allen, Morgan Soderberg, Jessica Donnelly, Caroline Douglas, Linda, Maria, and Amy D'Agrosa, and Daryn Stier.

Bliss

I actually remember feeling delight, at two o'clock in the morning, when the baby woke for his feed, because I so longed to have another look at him.

                           MARGARET DRABBLE

A love affair with our children starts the moment they are born. For some of us, it begins even earlier. The closeness of carrying a child in the womb makes separation seem strange.

Night feedings may be inconvenient. Yet we long for our child to awake just to get another look. Though we don't yet know the traits of her personality, she is like a close friend who has come a long distance to visit, and we want to stay up all night just to be together.

Nothing can compare to the bliss that surrounds a newborn and her mother.

In the sheltered simplicity of the first days after a baby is born, one sees again the magical closed circle, the miraculous sense of two people existing only for each other.

                        ❧ ANNE MORROW LINDBERGH

Something happens when our baby first comes home. The magical circle closes around us, strengthening the bond we share. We again feel the mutual love that brought us together and created our child. Our house becomes a home imbued with bliss. Our eyes speak with the vows of our hearts. Although we and our mate are beginning a new journey with a third little person, for a time, we experience "the miraculous sense of two people existing only for each other."

Maybe I can allow myself to bask in this time of "sheltered simplicity" as it will never be repeated.

The other day I accidentally caught Lily's skin in one of her snaps. She screamed so loud I felt like a mother-from-hell.

👍 LEE DURLAND

*B*eing a new mom is not easy. We have to learn everything by doing. The problem is, we're learning on a tiny, sensitive being who yelps at the first indications of discomfort. No wonder we feel insecure and tentative. We're fearful our infant might not survive our mistakes.

It helps to remember that confidence building is exactly that—a building process. We learn from our mistakes, and slowly lay a foundation of successes. We need to be patient with ourselves and remember that we have our own pace. We can't go any faster than we're capable of going. If we rush, we make mistakes and that will undermine our successes.

It took two to three days for my milk to come in. Wouldn't it have been nice if my confidence came in with it?

The dignity of the artist lies in his duty of keeping awake the sense of wonder in the world.

         ❧ G.K. CHESTERTON

*T*o infants, the ordinary is extraordinary. From the moment they are born, they are full of wonder. Like artists, they study each intricate detail of our face, discovering every freckle and line. They're seeing the world for the first time; everything is fresh, everything is an object of wonder: a piece of carpet lint, a button on a blouse, a strand of hair.

Remember how you felt when you first saw a ferris wheel? The pink and yellow lights of a carousel? A three-tiered cake with icing roses? When we see the world through our little one's eyes, we experience anew our own childlike sense of wonder.

Wonder is not reserved for children; they help to awaken it in us.

Lying in bed would be an altogether perfect and supreme experience if only one had a colored pencil long enough to draw on the ceiling.

        ❦ G.K. CHESTERTON

*F*orget the colored pencil! Just lying in bed would be "an altogether perfect experience." How long has it been? What's it like? Can't remember?

When we're finally organized enough to hire a babysitter or ask a friend to watch our child, we're too out of practice to enjoy the simple experience of doing nothing. We spend the entire time worrying about our baby. We can't relax. Separation anxiety is not only for babies; mothers have it, too.

By allowing myself some quiet time to be alone and relax, I'm improving the quality of time I spend with my child.

Excuse me, what did you ask me?
Did I ask you a question?
I think so, but I can't remember.

> 🍼 TWO POSTPARTUM WOMEN TRYING TO HAVE A
> CONVERSATION.

O ne of the first things a new mother notices after delivery is memory loss. The change is so sudden, it's frightening. We feel grossly inarticulate as we struggle to form a sentence. "Just a few weeks ago, I was an intelligent person," we hear ourselves telling friends. "I think all my brain cells came out with the afterbirth!"

Those of us who are accustomed to managing a full schedule are especially shaken by this uninvited occurrence. Were we ever organized, or was that simply an illusion?

Eventually, the reasons for our bodies' actions become clear. We see that it is for our own good. Mother Nature wants us to reduce our awareness of external demands so we can focus solely on our child.

May I trust that my body knows best during this delicate time. My loss of memory will not last forever.

Ideas won't keep: something must be done about them.

        🪱 ALFRED NORTH WHITEHEAD

*W*hat our creativity calls out to us cannot wait. The images and voices of the muse are inspired *in the moment.* Trying to hold it back is like trying to prevent gravity from pulling on the ocean's tides.

Creativity is not designed for fitting into a mother's busy day, nor is it convenient. It may disrupt our sleep, invade our dreams, and distract our thoughts until we give it expression. If we try to stave off its advances and ask it to wait until the children leave home, we may find ourselves stranded without inspiration.

Listening to my creative impulse and expressing it eases my creative tension and enhances my life.

The thing about having a baby is that thereafter you have it.

&back; QUENTIN CRISP

*E*veryone of us knew this when we decided to become parents. Then why are we so taken aback when the magnitude of our commitment begins to sink in?

All the serene and heavenly images of motherhood depicted in paintings and advertisements shatter. Our infant is not beatific and is rarely still. He has three expressions: starting to cry, crying, and just finished crying. We have only three expressions: blank stare, terror, and blank stare. We're not even sure we will survive the first few months of basic training.

Just when we think we're doomed, things improve. We can detect mood changes before they occur; we learn how to meet our little one's needs; we detect a pattern to his behavior. Holding him tight, we decide to keep him, and the minute we do that, something changes. We begin to worry about his teen years!

I'm in this for life, not a life sentence.

He knew by experience that he absorbed everything. . . . It was as if memory congealed somewhere, then suddenly, through some mechanism of association, appeared before his eyes with blinding intensity.

&EVA LUNA (ISABEL ALLENDE)

*B*abies are a "mechanism of association," awakening both the joy and pain of our youth. Our early experiences return to us with "blinding intensity" as the past collides with the present. We may be filled with the same emotions we felt when the event first took place. In some cases, our pain is asking to be healed and released. In others, our joy confirms the rich texture of our lives. We may shed tears, giggle, or reflect with pain on lessons learned. Each time an experience returns to us, we have the opportunity to bring it more fully into who we are.

My feelings are a part of me. When I embrace my feelings, I embrace myself.

Everyone has a right to my opinion.

YOGI BERRA

*W*here is it written that babies are public property? The minute we leave our homes, we're showered with unsolicited advice. Everyone from the banker to the toll booth operator has an opinion! One mother told me about an experience she had while still in the hospital. "My baby wasn't but two minutes old, and a nurse said to me, 'You don't need to feed her every time she cries, you'll spoil her.' Can you believe it?!" Of course I can—all mothers can. It's as though the mere sight of a baby forces people to rattle off childrearing theories to unsuspecting mothers. It doesn't seem to matter that the child is a perfect stranger to them, someone they know nothing about.

I can't control what others say, but I can use my humor to deflect it.

Compared to other feelings, love is an elemental cosmic force weaving a disguise of meekness . . . . It is not a state of mind; it is the foundation of the universe.

          ❧ BORIS PASTERNAK

When we first look into the eyes of our new-born baby, we are often overwhelmed by the intensity of the love we feel. We may even wonder if we have ever felt genuine love before. It is in these moments that we transcend the boundaries of our everyday existence and experience love as "the foundation of the universe." Although the power of these moments may fade, or simply be swallowed up by external demands, they are always accessible to us. We have only to reflect on the birth of our child.

When I feel I have no more love to give, I must remember I can tap into that cosmic force I've experienced through love.

These are the times that try men's [sic] *souls . . .*
🎗 THOMAS PAYNE

*B*eing a new mother can try a woman's soul. Those of us who make the decision to have a child usually discover that we got more than we bargained for. No matter how many crises we've endured, including floods and earthquakes, motherhood is harder. The cumulative upsets that can be generated in one day are certainly trying. Baby won't go down for a nap even though he has that vacant look in his eyes; he won't take a bottle; he gets jealous when we talk on the phone. He arches his back in a full-bodied "no." Everything is maddening, and we trudge through the day hoping things will improve. Our only solace comes from knowing that it can't continue like this forever.

Motherhood is hard. Luckily, it's not always as hard as it is during its earliest stages.

We seldom stop to think how many peoples' lives are entwined with our own. It is a form of selfishness to imagine that every individual can operate on his own or can pull out of the general stream and not be missed.

               ✑ IVY BAKER PRIEST

*H*aving a baby usually "pulls us out of the general stream." For a time, it's impossible to leave the house to see a movie. Our phone conversations are interrupted. We're too exhausted to write a letter to completion. As a result, contact with our friends is limited.

When our friends express their desire to see us, it's easy to feel guilty. We feel pressured by their requests. Why can't they understand?

Our true friends do understand. They don't have to like it but they understand. They accommodate our "special needs" and they keep their expectations low until we adjust to the changes in our lives.

My presence is greatly missed. Have I told my friends how much I miss them?

Soldiering Through

The toughest job you'll ever love.

U.S. ARMY SLOGAN

Motherhood makes boot camp look like an ice cream social. We've seen soiled diapers that would bring a grown man to his knees! While soldiers tote the evenly distributed weight of a pack, we haul a wiggling child. We lift him 100,000 times a day. We lug him and his tricycle home from the park. Now, that's what I call physical endurance!

While soldiers complain about getting up at the crack of dawn, our day can start at any time. Bleary-eyed we must still buy groceries and drive a car. We are on the front lines everyday and have only our inner strength as replacements. We can't resign. We love our job—we may not always like it, but we love it. We're not gluttons for punishment. We're the proud, the brave, the Moms.

Sometimes we feel as though we've enlisted in one of the toughest campaigns imaginable. Aren't we glad we can laugh?

. . . . all that was lost in oblivion regained precise dimensions . . . .

🐚 EVA LUNA (ISABEL ALLENDE)

Caring for a newborn is like being a first year college student. The onslaught of information is dizzying. Each day there are comprehensive tests and pop quizzes. There's so much we must quickly learn about our new baby. We stop watching the news. We are too tired to absorb what is going on around us. We forget to eat. We are "lost in oblivion" as the months rush by in a "baby blur."

Then, almost miraculously, our head clears. We no longer feel dazed; our thoughts aren't fuzzy and random. Words that have eluded us for the past several months—like "car" "book" "spoon"—now return with fluid consistency. Finals are over and life can resume.

The state of oblivion is only a transient phase of motherhood. The "precise dimensions" do return.

Yes, it hurts when buds burst, there is pain when something grows.

꙳ KARIN BOYE

 shed tears of joy when Alexander first crawled across the floor. I clapped and cheered. Moments later, I realized that life with him would never be the same. His baby days were over, he would soon be a toddler. Then I cried again as a sense of loss washed over me.

We provide support and encouragement for our little ones. We help them learn to crawl, to walk, and to stand. Yet, with every accomplishment, there is a twinge of sadness. Maybe our children no longer need us? They do need us, but they must keep growing, developing, changing.

Happy moments are often laced with sadness as my emotions embrace the changes in my life.

Solitude is un-American.

🖒 ERICA JONG

𝓜 others are notorious for being guilt-ridden whenever they spend time alone. There is always something or someone else that needs our attention. It also doesn't help to live in a society that places a disproportionate amount of value on busyness. We are suspect if we actually enjoy being alone, away from the crowd. Yet, perhaps more than anyone, mothers need solitude. It's vital to our well-being.

When was the last time I was completely alone? I probably need to schedule a date with myself soon. What about today?

Grief melts away
Like snow in May
As if there were no such cold thing.

🍂 GEORGE HERBERT

No matter how much time we take to prepare, childbirth dramatically changes our lives overnight.

It is only natural to long for "life before baby." We think of the freedom we had. We could read a book until we finished it, hop on a plane to Paris, or throw a lavish dinner party. Whether or not we actually did these things is irrelevant. It's the feeling that we *could* have done them that causes us to grieve for our lost freedom.

It's normal to feel confined after life-with-baby begins. It doesn't mean we don't love our child. It doesn't mean we don't enjoy being a mother.

I have given up some things to be a mom.
But they are not gone from me forever.

The majority of husbands remind me of an orangutan trying to play the violin.

🎵 HONORE DE BALZAC

Many of us thought the same thing when we saw our husband handling his first dirty diaper. But let's face it, we too look pretty clumsy when we're first learning how to do something. Our movements with a new baby are awkward. We feel unsure. We stumble through each step. "Will I ever strike the right chord?" "Will I ever be graceful?" "Will there ever come a time when I won't wince at myself?"

With patience and practice, we learn to feel comfortable as parents. We learn to take our "sour notes" in stride. In time, we make beautiful music together— dirty diapers and all!

Just because I peek at the sheet music every once in a while doesn't mean I can't play first fiddle.

Trust your heart.... Never deny it a hearing.
It is the kind of house oracle that often foretells the
most important.

☞ BALTHASAR GRACIAN

*A*lexander was just seven months old. "The books said" that he should have been sleeping *five* hours by then. My husband and I were at our wits' end, and lack of sleep was skewing our judgment and perception. We listened to the warnings of experts: "He'll develop insomnia if you don't make changes now... You're only letting him manipulate you when you allow him to sleep with you," and we decided to ignore our hearts' pleas and let him cry. It was agonizing to listen to his screams. This was the first time in his entire life that mommy or daddy didn't come to him after he started crying.

The next day he was different, withdrawn and sullen. I ached inside; it pained me to see him this way. Finally, when I could still the voices in my head and listen to the wisdom of my heart, clarity returned. Alexander's trust was more important than our sleep.

When I don't listen to the voice of my heart, I make unwise choices.

"No"

Whenever I say "yes," he says "no," I say "stop," he says "go."

Sometimes it seems as though our child wants the opposite of whatever we want. During certain phases, it might even seem as though he has a personal vendetta against us.

While it is easy to see certain actions as a personal affront, they are not. Like all of us, children need to establish their own limits and boundaries. They are trying to test their independence, to gain further understanding about the world. And, like most of us, they are a little anxious about it.

Our childrens' resistance might be their way of telling us that we need to back off and give them room to explore. Perhaps we interfere a bit too often because *we* feel anxious. Maybe we need to ask ourselves if *our* fears are restricting *their* behavior. If so, then we are not respecting our child as an individual, an individual who is different from us.

May I always support my child's growth and not thwart his challenges with my fears.

Mine, O thou lord of life, send my roots rain.
                                    ❧GERARD MANLEY HOPKINS

*B*eing a mother is one of the most rewarding and most draining things we will ever do. When we consider the requirements of the job, it's not surprising that this is so. We're not only giving our time, attention, and energy, we're giving ourselves. To do that day after day takes a great deal of inner strength.

It is essential for us to "send our roots rain," to replenish our vital source or we'll find our supply running dangerously low. For some, that means prayer or meditation. For others, a walk in nature connects us to life again. It doesn't matter which route we choose as long as it brings us closer to ourselves and our inner strength.

When my soul feels parched, I need to drench it with the source that best renews my spirit.

"Carpe diem"—seize the day

✎ HORACE

This B.C. Latin poet definitely speaks to contemporary moms.

I leap out of bed.
Baby is fed.
I throw on my clothes.
I wipe the kid's nose.
I pull out some cash.
I step on the gas.
Baby's secured in the cart.
I march through the mart.
I mustn't dawdle.
I feed baby his bottle.
I finish one chore.
I leave the store.
I look at my list.
I give baby a kiss.
I could fall to the floor, but...
There's more, more, more!

Seize the day—the battle cry for moms who want to get things done!

An ounce of mother is worth a ton of priest.
　　　　　　　　　　　　　　SPANISH PROVERB

We *are* the experts. Although we may not hold lofty degrees, and we may not have written books about our research, we are accomplished in our field. Why? Because mothers are creative and resourceful and they'll try innumerable things to find what really works. In short, mothers are the "queens of the eclectic." We listen to all the varieties and approaches available, then we stir them around in our thoughts like a big pot of stew and out comes a new creation.

Mothers realize that children are very different. One theory, even a good one, is not fitting for every child. And we should know, we've tried them all!

Mothers have the wisdom of experience. So, next time I want solid advice, I'll ask another mom.

Nowadays, I ignore my body's signals when they tell me I'm getting sick because I hate the thought of not being able to lie in bed.

🔖 NEW MOTHER

*G*etting sick while caring for a baby is awful. We'd like to say to our infant: "Go ahead and dress yourself, you know where your clothes are, and go ahead and feed yourself, you know where the food is kept, and go ahead and play, you know where your toys are." However, we can't. We have to rough it.

No matter how lousy we feel, the show must go on. There is still a little person who depends on us for her care. We don't know how we get well without lying in bed but somehow we do.

It must be motherhood that makes me so resilient. Either that or I wasn't as sick as I thought!

Sex is nobody's business except the three people involved.

🖐 UNKNOWN

*M*aking love with a newborn in the house can be an arousing experience, though unfortunately, not for us. First of all, it is difficult to get in the mood when we're exhausted. Second, it isn't easy to concentrate on sex with one ear tuned into listening to the baby's breathing. Third, we may not feel particularly attractive, especially if we haven't lost the weight we put on during pregnancy. Then, it seems inevitable, that just as we get caught up in the throes of passion, our baby wakes up screaming. When this happens, we have to change gears. Often, by the time we get baby back to sleep, we've lost what little interest we had in the first place.

With all these hurdles to overcome, it's no wonder my sex life is grounded like a plane that's missing a starboard engine.

Mother #1: Robert started crawling before he was six months old.
Mother #2: Stephen is in the 90th percentile in height.

*W*hen we compare our children, their self-esteem suffers. We are placing them in competition with other children because *we* feel insecure about their differences. When we worry that our child won't be tall enough, or smart enough, or athletic enough, he ends up feeling that he is not good enough.

To foster self-esteem and instill a healthy self-concept, it is essential to let our children know we love them the way they are—unconditionally. Instead of focusing on mistakes and failures, or differences from others, we accept who they are and encourage their strengths.

Self-esteem doesn't come from "being the best," it comes from valuing the best one can be.

Patience has its limits. Take it too far, and it's cowardice.

                       ✒ GEORGE JACKSON

"*Mother*" and "patience" are practically synonymous. However, mothers can be patient to the point where it's cowardice.

Some of us suspend our own creative endeavors until the children grow up. We think we are being virtuous by supplanting our needs by those of our children when actually, we are avoiding our own life. Others of us allow our husbands to do less than their share of child-rearing because we don't want to rock the boat and be accused of nagging.

Whenever we take our patience too far, we are probably afraid of something—standing up for ourselves, taking responsibility for our lives, initiating change, or taking a risk—and that is cowardice, not patience.

There's a fine line between patience and cowardice. Learning to recognize when I have crossed that line is part of being an adult and a mother.

*Whenever we take a trip, we have to enlist the help
of thirteen sherpas, a chauffeur, two maids and a
nanny—and that's only for the baby's luggage.*
✎ GINGER HINCHMAN

here's no such thing as "traveling light" with a
baby. Every item is essential: the stroller, the
backpack, the diaper bag, the portable crib, suitcases
for clothes and toys, and the video camera. We need
the help of professionals just to get to the airport!

Once we've boarded the plane, we need a traveling
circus to keep our infant entertained, then a restraint
system to hold her down while we eat. Otherwise,
we'll be sandwiched between two grouchy passengers while our baby grabs at our tray. Inevitably, after
the meal, our little one fills her pants. And we must
squeeze past passengers and into the narrow lavatory
to change her.

Yes, traveling with an infant adds a new dimension.
We still have to do everything we do at home. Only
when we travel, we do it in the air.

It's not just a trip, it's an adventure.

*The baby has learned to know and love you better
than anyone else and now he wants you all the time
and all to himself.... His ideal would be your
continual presence and constant attention.*

❧ PENELOPE LEACH

As mothers, our tie to our infants is like no other. When they're sick, they want mom to hold them. When they fall face first into the carpet, only mom's embrace will do. When they find a "treasure" on the floor, they want mom's mouth to pop it into.

These demonstrations of love are wonderful. However, when others besides our baby are also clamoring for our attention, we feel we are being spread too thin. An older child needs us; a friend telephones; our partner desires closeness. As much as we'd like to, it's impossible to respond to everyone all the time.

**I would like to be as attentive with my baby as my
baby is with me, but I can't and that's okay.
I give what I can, and that will have to be enough.**

Women who miscalculate are called mothers.

                         ABIGAIL VANBUREN

others miscalculate when we underestimate the talents of our child. When we think we've got them figured out, they surprise us. "Don't worry, he's not tall enough to reach the table." Down come the dishes and the lace tablecloth. "She couldn't possibly pull herself up on the couch." The lamp crashes to the floor.

Another way mothers miscalculate: we overestimate our ability to get things done. "After work, I'll straighten up the kitchen, watch the news, and write a few thank you notes." We get home from work, eat, put the baby to bed, forget to brush our teeth, and wake up on the nursery floor at midnight. Or, "Let's drive into San Francisco and have a picnic by the ocean." By the time the children shower and get dressed, and we remember to make "just one quick call," no one has the energy to put the baby in the car seat and drive across the bridge.

Miscalculating is part of being a mother. Why should I stop when I'm so good at it!

*Beware of allowing a tactless word, rebuttal,
a rejection to obliterate the whole sky.*

🖎 ANAIS NIN

New mothers are targets for criticism. We're
vulnerable, nervous, and afraid we might do
the wrong thing. This is when others, including
members of our own family, strike. They think
they're helping when, in fact, they are attacking us at
a fragile time in our lives. The criticism stings and if
we're having a bad day, it can temporarily "obliterate
the sky."

As we become more confident and self-assured, the
careless words of others don't affect us as much. We
listen with a discerning ear ignoring insensitive com-
ments about us or our parenting style. Occasionally,
we'll feel strong enough to openly disagree with what
is said. But, if we are wise, we will spend the extra
energy on our child rather than on those who need to
be set straight.

**When I feel vulnerable, it is difficult to protect
myself from criticism. When I feel confident and
strong, criticism is a weak foe.**

Fulfillment

The tedious days were filled with miracles. When a baby first looks at you; when it gets excited at seeing a ray of light and like a dog pawing a gleam, tries to capture it in his hand; or when it laughs that deep, unselfconscious gurgle; or when it cries and you pick it up and it clings sobbing to you, saved from some terrible shadow moving across the room, or a loud bang in the street, or perhaps, already, a bad dream: then you are—happy is not the precise word—filled.

🐾 MARILYN FRENCH

*T*he fulfillment of motherhood is not a steady, blissful state. It is a responsibility-filled vocation permeated by an ineffable joy and love. Our hard work is rewarded with daily miracles as we witness the growth and development of a unique human being. Our frustrations are obliterated by gurgles and hugs, small gestures and toothless grins.

Our babies don't make us a more complete person. But they do fill us with their presence, and inspire us with their grand accomplishments: sucking on toes, rolling over, sitting up. They open us to love and help us to see the extraordinary in seemingly mundane events.

If I receive the everyday miracles as eagerly as I received my swaddled new born, I will be filled.

*To be a housewife is . . . a difficult, a wrenching,
sometimes ungrateful job if it's looked on as only a
job. Regarded as a profession, it is the noblest as it is
the most ancient of the catalogue. Let none persuade
us differently or the world will be lost indeed.*

                                 ❧ PHYLLIS MCGINLEY

*I*n recent years, being a housewife has gotten a
bad rap. We reacted to unfair restrictions and a
lack of options. Unfortunately, the baby got thrown
out with the bath water. In our haste to make sweeping changes, we discredited one of the noblest and
most ancient professions around.

Fortunately, we have learned not to generalize. We
no longer view womanhood in such black and white
terms. A woman's life does not have to be confined to
only one domain. We've redefined success in a way
that values *all* the professions of women.

**If I respect myself and the choices I make, I can
respect the choices other women make.**

Sleep

People who say they sleep like a baby usually don't have one.

🍼 LEO J. BURKE

No mother was responsible for the old saying: "I slept like a baby." We know better. Babies, especially newborns, rarely sleep like "a rock." More often than not, their days and nights are reversed. Let's face it, our sleep patterns are at odds with our babies'! Babies go into deep sleep for a short period, move into lighter sleep, and often awaken during this time. Adults, on the other hand, gradually move into deep sleep as the night progresses. Then slowly, we come out of it. Babies sleep lightly because their survival depends on it. Their systems alert them when they are hungry, wet, cold, or hot. With all these disruptions, it's no wonder they don't sleep long, and neither do we.

The only thing better than a sleeping baby is a sleeping mother.

Change

It's always something!
    ROSEANNA ROSEANNA DANNA (GILDA RADNER)

*D*oesn't it seem like every time we try to change things to make our lives a little easier, we get undermined? For instance, if I try to alter my son's sleeping schedule so his daddy and I can have more time to ourselves, he starts teething. And, of course, the child psychology books say we should never try to impose a new pattern on a child when there is a disruption in his life such as teething or travel, or... So, I say to myself, "Self, we'll just wait until his gums don't hurt so much. Then, we'll make our move." Of course, when I finally develop a strategy and am about to implement it, he's developed his first illness! Maybe by the time he's eighteen....

Let's face it, we may chart the course, but our babies will take their own route.

Healing

The human heart does not stay away too long from that which hurt it most. There is a return journey to anguish that few of us are released from making.
　◆ LILLIAN SMITH

*I*f we haven't worked through the hurts of our childhood, we now have the chance.

Having a child ripens our awareness of our own youth and helps us to heal. As we embrace our new role as a mother, an inner strength emerges that enables us to handle whatever feelings and memories come up. At times, we may feel overwhelmed and have difficulty separating our own inner struggles from our child's. But this is all part of the process. The human heart strives for wholeness. When it journeys back into the pain of our lives, it does so with the intention of healing us.

I will accept the gift of healing when my heart and mind are ready.

Babies do not have a fixed quota of love to give, so having more than one person who is 'special' to him does not deprive a baby's mother of anything.

PENELOPE LEACH

It's natural to feel jealous and threatened by our babies' relationships with others. But our babies don't have a fixed quota of love, nor is their love an either/or proposition. We hold a special place in their hearts. They love us at their core and from there, they extend their love to others.

Mothers who work, either by choice or necessity, are especially prone to possessiveness. When we must rely on someone else to care for our child, it's easy to feel replaced. Mothers sometimes even feel betrayed as though our baby's caring for someone else means they no longer love us. However, our unique bond with our child is unbreakable. In the evenings and on weekends, whenever we have time with our baby, we can nurture this bond.

These feelings are telling me that I miss being close with my baby. Perhaps I can take some extra time to be with her today.

*Parenting, at its best, comes as naturally as laughter.
It is automatic, involuntary, unconditional love.*

❧ SALLY JAMES

e've all experienced days when our mothering flows "as naturally as laughter," when we are "at our best." Nothing, not even overdue bills, interferes with our primary focus: our child. We're relaxed with our baby: our responses are open and spontaneous. We're confident about our parenting skills, and we're not distracted by worries. We know our little one is loved and well cared for.

It's tempting to try to figure out exactly what we do on these particular days so that we can re-create them. The truth is, these days are gifts visited upon us—we can not make them happen.

It's unrealistic to expect to be at our very best every day. I must remember not to blame myself when I have days that are other than my best.

Confusion

My life feels like a grade school band: scattered with no discernible rhythm.

❧ ANONYMOUS

*W*omen are very good at diffusing their attention. Like conductors, we orchestrate life's many details. We keep appointments, remember to return phone calls, and save holiday recipes. We remember to feed the cat and dog, and we even remember to rinse out our panty hose before we go to sleep.

When we add a baby to our list, it's not surprising that we feel confused, fragmented, and overwhelmed. We still have to do all of these things, and care full time for an infant! At first, our lives are full of discord. We're out of tune. Then, slowly, we learn how to strike a more harmonious balance.

When I feel like I'm scattered without rhythm, it's time to stop and take a moment to re-group.

Dependency invites encroachment.

          🖎 PATRICIA MEYER SPACKS

s our children gradually become aware of their own power and abilities, they go through periods of intense anxiety. They are making discoveries about themselves that are often overwhelming. They realize they are separate from us. They are driven toward independence, yet they want to be assured of our continual presence in their lives.

By establishing boundaries for our children, we give them a solid foundation from which they can venture out, certain of our love. When we fail to set limits, we give them more power than they can handle. Instead of instilling a sense of security, we undermine their efforts toward independence.

Setting boundaries for myself and my child behooves us both.

It is hard to fight an enemy who has outposts in your head.

❧ SALLY KEMPTON

others can be their own worst enemies. As women, we learn that motherhood is sacred. But does that mean we have to be perfect angels? More often than not, what we demand of ourselves is someone who is superhuman. And, no matter how hard we try, we can't meet these unrealistic standards. We set ourselves up to fail.

Even when we manage to catch ourselves playing this destructive mental game, we find that the messages of others have established outposts in our heads: "A good mother never shouts . . . . A good mother never loses her temper." On and on they go. When we try to please everyone, we end up pleasing no one, least of all ourselves.

It is difficult to fight an enemy who has outposts in my head, but it can be done! Awareness is the first step.

Kids, yeah, I like kids . . . medium rare.

✑W.C. FIELDS

here's no doubt about it, children of all ages
can get on our nerves. Even infants can push us
to our limit. It doesn't matter if it's incessant crying or
constant motion, there comes a time when we feel
we can't take it anymore. When we find ourselves
wanting our babies "medium rare," it's a signal. That's
the time to take time out for ourselves. We need to
take a deep breath.

When I feel an edge to my humor, I need a break.

Imagination is not just fantasy, but an actual faculty by which we apprehend the world.

🖎 DAVID WHYTE

As adults, we often fail to call upon the creative energies of the imagination. We feel we must constantly focus on our parental responsibilities or chaos will erupt. Perhaps we view it as a luxury we cannot afford. When this happens, our imagination shrinks and we lose a valuable perspective.

Fortunately, children have fertile imaginations. There is no better way to stimulate our own imaginings than to listen to the colorful "babble" of our little ones.

My imagination is a gift. It helps me see the magic possibilities available to me.

I fall to pieces . . .

🎵 PATSY CLINE

I started listening to the songs of Patsy Cline at about six and a half months. Not surprisingly, *I Fall To Pieces* soon became my favorite tune. The dramatic twangs and soulful swoons captured my hormonal mood swings unlike any other music. They replenished my vitality like water on a wilted flower. But I was embarrassed to tell anyone. I was a closet Patsy fan until several other moms admitted they listened to her songs whenever they could. Only Patsy can clear up those baby day blues.

Patsy, you're singin' our song . . . .

The position of women in a society provides an exact measure of the development of that society.

◕ GUSTAV GEIGER

*T*oday we live in a society where the virtues of motherhood are given a tremendous amount of lip service, especially around election time. Yet, as we all know, the United States continues to be one of the few industrialized nations that does not provide adequate child care facilities, or parental leave. In fact, the President recently vetoed a bill which would insure job security after three months of unpaid maternity leave!

It makes us wonder how much of what mothers do is valued by our society. Even if we don't think about it on a daily basis, we may feel it on a more subtle level. Fortunately, mothers are resourceful and creative. We take pride in what we do. We find a way to meet the real needs of motherhood while we wait for the rest of the country to catch up!

I am proud of the mothering I do and I can create change at any level I choose: at home, at work, or in the political arena.

Fear has a smell, as love does.

✍ MARGARET ATWOOD

*H*ave you ever noticed how your child looks at you to see if he's hurt? When he takes a spill, he immediately checks mom's reaction. Sure, he can feel his own pain, but he's also learning about fear.

Just as our actions teach our children about love, they also teach them fear. Those of us who are uneasy with the expression of emotions teach our child to be fearful of anger, sadness, and even love. If we are frightened by water, our child senses it. So instead of enjoying the freedom of moving weightlessly through the water, he learns to fear it. Our children sense our fears; they smell them. And the ones we have not released, we pass on.

I can overcome my fears if I understand and accept their source.

Such a knot of little purposeful nature!
         ❧ RICHARD EBERHART

*T*here comes a time when our baby is no longer content to observe the world; he wants to be part of it. As a visiting friend remarked: "He looks like he's on a mission!"

Almost overnight, our child reaches a level of mastery with his body and is determined to exercise his newly acquired talents. Passion is his driving force. Nothing is safe from his grasp.

Mothers also need to pursue our passions. It doesn't matter whether we choose to do that in the realm of motherhood, work, or other aspects of our lives. What does matter is that we feel passionate about whatever it is we're doing. Without passion, our lives feel empty and unfulfilled.

True passion is an expression of my deepest, most genuine self. It is the language of the soul.

*My obstetrician was so dumb that when I gave birth he
forgot to cut the cord. For a year that kid followed me
everywhere.*

✑ JOAN RIVERS

*M*any of us are sure we have the same obstetrician because our kid follows us everywhere! Like a blood hound, our baby even tracks us
to the bathroom. If we tell him to wait outside the
door, he howls like an abandoned pup. He frequently
sleeps in our bed, and has the audacity to hog the
covers!

No wonder mothers come to use the proverbial
"we." "We" can't go out today because it's too cold.
"We" have an appointment with the doctor on Thurs-
day. "We" are very excited about "our" new toy.
Privacy has become a thing of the past. If we could
only stop and see the humor in our constant
attachment. Someday in the not too distant future,
we'll probably miss the company.

**It could be worse: we could be followed by some-
one we *didn't* like!**

*Mimi says I have a special voice for storytelling,
a voice that, although mine, also seems to belong to
someone else, as if it issued from the earth to rise
through my body.*

✏ EVA LUNA (ISABEL ALLENDE)

*C*hildren afford us the opportunity to find the ancient voice of the storyteller inside ourselves. When we weave a tale, we not only pass on valuable information about ourselves and our family history, we also stimulate our young listeners' minds and send them on a journey.

Our children are not the only ones to benefit. Our stories often convey deeper parts of ourselves, as significant events we may have forgotten find their way into our stories. Occasionally, we might even experience the voice of Mother Earth as her words flow from our lips.

May I always be open to the sacred power of the storyteller who dwells within me.

Sometimes, when one person is missing, the whole world seems depopulated.

🐚 ALPHONSE DE LAMARTINE

*D*uring the early months of our baby's life, we feel alone and isolated whenever our partner leaves for work. We dread the sound of the door closing, separating us from the outside world. It's irrelevant that we can leave if we want. The fact is, we *feel* as if we can't. We feel locked in, cut off from everything familiar. It's as though the parameters of our world end at the front door. Homebound, we wonder if anyone else exists. We crave conversation with another adult human being.

When, at the end of the day, our partner returns, what's the first thing he says? "I sure wish I didn't have to go to work so I could stay home with the baby." We scratch our heads in disbelief. Perhaps the grass always does seem greener on the other side of the fence.

Staying home alone with a newborn infant can be an isolating experience. I must actively seek out the company of other mothers.

*You will do foolish things, but do them with
enthusiasm.*

~COLETTE

Mothers often take themselves too seriously.
After all, we're shaping the life of another
human being. Nothing could be more important than
that.

Certainly, who we are and how we act has a profound effect on our children. But does that mean that
everything we do must be done correctly? (Whatever
"correctly" is?) If we start from the premise that we
will do foolish things, then we can do them with
enthusiasm and add spice and spontaneity to our days.

As mothers quickly learn, there is a big difference
between foolish things and harmful ones.

Foolishness can be fun!

There was no need to do any housework at all. After the first four years, the dirt doesn't get any worse.
                                          ✑ QUENTIN CRISP

*O*ne of the ironies of being a full-time mother is that we rarely have time to do anything else. Both we and our husbands underestimate the amount of time it takes to care for an infant. So we're both surprised when he returns home at the end of the day and the house is still a mess.

There *is* only so much time in a day, and caring for an infant takes most of it. And since no mother is going to neglect her baby to dust—some domestic chores simply have to go! At first, we think we'll never be able to tolerate the accumulation of dirt and grime. But after a while, living in a less than clean house becomes an accepted fact of life.

Housework may not be as high on my list of priorities as I once thought.

Rest

Rest is not idleness, and to lie sometimes on the grass under the trees on a summer's day, listening to the murmur of water, or watching the clouds float across the sky, is by no means a waste of time.

❧ SIR J. LUBBOCK

Too often we use our free time to do household chores, or answer letters or finish up work from the office. This is not rest.

Many of us think that if we're not watching the baby, we're relaxing. Well, this just ain't so. Mothers need genuine rest. We need time to simply be with ourselves, and we can do this in a variety of ways. We can take a hot bath, stroll through the park, or gently rock ourselves in a rocking chair. It doesn't matter how we get in touch with ourselves, but it's important that we do. Otherwise, like the government, we will soon be operating at a large deficit.

When I take time to rest, I am not wasting time. I am enjoying it.

My mother didn't breast-feed me. She said she liked me as a friend.

              ❧ RODNEY DANGERFIELD

Some of us are frightened by intimacy, even with our own children. Perhaps our own parents had difficulty demonstrating their feelings toward us, or were emotionally unavailable. Whatever the reason, we avoid physical closeness.

Babies need touch as much as they need food and clothing, perhaps more. Those of us who are uncomfortable with kisses and caresses might find a new start with our innocent new babe. They don't want to be "just friends," and they won't settle for less than the best we can give.

My baby's loving way comes so naturally to her. If I am less afraid of intimacy, I can learn how to express love in return.

Hey, the way I figure it is this: If the kids are still alive by the time my husband comes home, I've done my job.

                   ✍ ROSEANNE ARNOLD

*W*e all have expectations about the kind of mother we'll be. Our stomachs balloon and we dream about rearranging our life-with-baby. We envision ourselves sewing outfits and baking bread. But once baby is born, our fantasies of "Little House on the Prairie" are consumed by brush fires. Every morning we face a long list of tasks: feed baby, burp baby, give baby a bath. Sometimes we enjoy doing these things, sometimes we don't. Nevertheless, we do learn to integrate them into our routines.

Of course, there will still be days when doing our best "ain't nothin' fancy." Like Roseanne, we'll feel we've done our job if the kids are still alive when our husband comes home!

I mustn't let high expectations run me into the ground. Sometimes being a "good enough" mother is very good indeed.

*It's pretty hard to be efficient without being
obnoxious.*

                              Kim Hubbard

others have to be efficient if they want to get anything done. We're coordinating the needs of so many individuals, often single-handedly, that we have to run a tight ship. Sometimes, however, we sound like a drill sergeant shouting orders.

At times this method is appropriate. However, if we rely on it too much, we become overbearing and obnoxious. When this happens, we don't feel good about ourselves. This is a good time to sit ourselves down and get clear about our priorities. We probably need to communicate our feelings to our spouse, and find ways to redistribute the load.

**If I always mow everyone down, I can't expect
them to feel that this is a team effort!**

Confidence

When he brought Jackson home I felt all alone. How was I to care for this tiny infant? My mind went blank. I couldn't remember anything the nurses had told me! I was sure I was doomed.

         ❧ JESSICA DONNELLY

*T*here is nothing stranger than bringing baby home, looking at him, then suddenly realizing that we don't have a clue as to what he likes and dislikes. We know he needs to eat and sleep and have his diapers changed, but how often and in what order? And we panic! Every bit of helpful information freezes in our brains. We have to rely on ourselves, and quite frankly, we'd rather do anything but that.

Then, one day, we accidentally bounce on the edge of the mattress and baby's tears dry up. Our confidence grows. We learn to distinguish between baby's cries for food, cuddles, and sleep. Again, our confidence grows. After numerous and painful tries, we get the breast pump to work. Day after day, the little things add up until our insecurities are overshadowed by our successes.

As my baby grows so does my confidence.

Nothing contributes so much to tranquilize the mind as a steady purpose—a point on which the soul may fix its intellectual eye.

🐚 MARY WOLLSTONECRAFT SHELLEY

others are easily distracted. Every morning we awaken to innumerable tasks and projects that we were unable to finish the previous day or the previous week. We become so frantic trying to complete a project that we try to do everything at once. We dress our infant, and on the way to the highchair, pick up dirty clothes off the floor. We start washing dishes as we prepare his meal, and as he eats, straighten out the piles of mail that have accumulated. Distracted, we jump from task to task, often forgetting what we had originally set out to do. Is it any wonder that our brains feel like mush?

We probably need to focus our minds by practicing singleness of purpose. What we chose to do is probably not as important as choosing to do only *one* thing.

I have become so accustomed to diffusing my attention that my mind lacks focus and direction. It's time to fix "my intellectual eye."

Absolute attention is prayer.

ONE WORLD, ONE PEOPLE

*I*t is easy to become scattered when there are so
many details to remember. Yet there are
moments when we are so completely focused on our
baby that we are one with him. We hold him close
offering a breast or a bottle. He looks up at us, and his
eyes hold ours in rapt attention. The intimacy is
intense, vibrant, and loving. Searching the face of this
new being, we try to fathom who he is. We almost
can't believe he is real.

As in prayer or meditation, these concentrated
moments of absolute attention bring us back to ourselves. They bring with them a deep sense of peace,
and a serenity that nourishes us.

**I must learn to quiet the distractions when I can;
otherwise I will scatter like leaves in the wind.**

Ef women want any rights more'n dey got, why don't dey jes' take 'em and not be talkin' about it.

            ❧ SOJOURNER TRUTH

Sojourner Truth, a nineteenth-century emancipated slave, understood why people had to fight for their rights. She realized that those in power are never going to "give permission" to those who want power. One must claim it for oneself.

Think about it. How many times have we had to challenge the existing authority, especially where our baby's welfare was concerned? Perhaps a physician discounts our diagnosis and, as a result, our child ends up in the emergency room. Maybe a prescribed medication is causing harmful side-effects and our doctor tells us we're "imagining" them.

When we're faced with crises, we can't spend too much time "talkin'," we've got to act. We can change doctors, change medication, do whatever is necessary—it's our right.

Challenging or disagreeing with the powers that be can be frightening, yet when the need is great, we can be assertive and act in our child's behalf.

I was raised in an abusive household. I want to break the cycle. I want to treat my child differently.
        👆KATHY FINNIGAN

Some of us come from abusive families. We know the pain this has created in our lives, and we don't want to inflict the same pain on our children. We are determined to be different, yet as we sometimes discover, determination alone may not be enough. Our reactions are so heavily ingrained that we strike out before we realize what we've done. Our guilt only makes us feel worse about ourselves and, in our pain, we strike out again. We may no longer feel victimized by our parents, but by the abusive behavior we've inherited.

The desire to change is not enough. I must find a new way to be.

Comparison

The ladies looked one another over with microscopic carelessness.

ARTHUR "BUGS" BAER

One of the most common things new mothers do is compare ourselves to other new mothers. We clandestinely scan another's figure and we compare it to our own. If she's thinner, we wonder how she lost weight so soon after the birth. We notice the circles under her eyes from lack of sleep. Are mine darker?

We use each other as measuring sticks. But what are we really measuring? Most likely, we're measuring our performance. We want to know how other mothers are coping with the stress of a newborn. To know if we're doing it right, we study all the postpartum indicators.

Unfortunately, we are looking in the wrong place. We are looking outside ourselves for answers that can only be found inside.

Comparing myself to others always makes me feel bad. Maybe, just for today, I can accept where I am.

The commonest fallacy among women is that simply having children makes one a mother—which is as absurd as believing that having a piano makes one a musician.

&Sydney J. Harris

In the age of "instant cereals" and "instant winners," it is tempting to believe that one can become an "instant mother." If we just buy all the right equipment, read a few "how-to" books, and decorate the extra bedroom . . . . Fortunately, it's not that simple.

Motherhood is not a passing phase, or a fad that we can simply put on and dispose of when we're tired of it. It requires a deep, personal commitment. It is not something we are necessarily good at. It may even be something we don't especially like. We may have to practice. We will probably have to accommodate new changes that are not always to our liking. It will take patience to grow into motherhood and mature into adults.

Becoming a mother is a process, not an event.

The important thing in acting is to be able to laugh and cry. If I have to cry, I think of my sex life. If I have to laugh, I think of my sex life.

✍ GLENDA JACKSON

*H*aving a little person who is constantly intimate with your wife can be very difficult for husbands. They feel left out and neglected. Why are their needs always being sacrificed for the baby's?

Most men don't always articulate this emotion to themselves or to us. All they know is that they are filled with this vague feeling of neediness and, as a result, their efforts to be close to us appear awkward and juvenile. Grabs and tweeks which used to be regarded as playful now annoy us. Their need for more meaningful contact feels like one more demand and we don't need the added pressure. We become indignant: "If he wants to be loving toward me, then why can't he wait until a more appropriate time?!"

Finding an appropriate time that is mutually agreeable will help me feel less mauled and more enthralled.

My spouse may not know how the way he's expressing his feelings is affecting me right now. I probably need to communicate my feelings to him.

Insecure in my new role, I was at odds with—and battered by—an ideal of the breezy, capable mother I assumed everyone else was. I could handle myself at important meetings, meet tough deadlines, argue fluently in French. Why couldn't I keep Cheerios off the kitchen floor?

🐌 LESLIE GEORGE

Many of us are successful in our work. We're accustomed to mastery over our environment. Then we have a baby and the rules change. Suddenly, we feel like neophytes. Different things are expected of us, but we're not sure what they are. We're sure every other mother is juggling her complicated life with finesse.

At some point, we realize the "other mother" doesn't really exist. That's when we can let ourselves off the hook. We discover that the floor is *supposed* to get messy. Laughter and spontaneity are requirements for the job. Planning is the exception, not the rule. There's only a minimum routine and even that changes every couple of weeks. Maybe we'll be good at this after all!

Like any new job, it takes awhile to learn the ropes. Expecting myself to be a pro right from the start shortcircuits this learning process.

Strength

We say we cannot bear our troubles but when we get to them we bear them.

　　　　　　　　　　　　　　❧ NING LAO T'AI'T'AI

The first several months following my C-section, I was so weak that I shook whenever I lifted Alexander for extended periods of time. The combination of surgery and sleep loss was debilitating. I kept thinking, "I'll never live through this! How will I last until he crawls?!" But somehow I made it through.

When we are in the midst of a personal crisis, we might not be gracious. In fact, we might be downright unpleasant to be around. During these times, it is important to keep things in perspective, even if that means taking the day one minute or even one second at a time. When we are experiencing a lot of inner turmoil, it is too easy to become embroiled in the future before it happens. And this prevents us from adequately dealing with what is at hand.

I am a strong woman or else I would not have made it this far. Let me draw on my strength moment by moment.

We set up two accounts for Alexander: A college fund and a therapy fund.

❧ BETH WILSON SAAVEDRA

New mothers are insecure. We're sure everything we're doing is wrong. Every slight mishap is damaging our child for life. No doubt we'll end up having to pay for years of therapy.

It's a fact, new mothers all believe that their child's discomforts are their fault and that these discomforts will lead to deep emotional scars. If our infant cries a lot, it's because we ate the wrong foods while we were pregnant. If he is restless and agitated, it's because we are not providing a soothing enough environment. If he hates his car seat, it's because he feels abandoned.

We're totally neurotic until we finally realize that we are not infallible. We are human beings and as such, we are not perfect.

I am a good mother. I will never be a perfect one.

After my daughter was born, I had to give some things up. You know, I don't really miss them.

RITA AVERY

eing forced to simplify our lives can be an illuminating experience. We find out what is important to us. We make choices about who we want to spend time with and we decide how and where we want to spend our energy.

We learn to say no. And we view our obligations differently, knowing we'll never be able to please everyone. We make decisions based on the needs and wants of ourselves and our family instead of on the expectations of others.

When I make choices based on what is meaningful to me, I am choosing to live a meaningful life.

The worst tempered people I've ever met were people who knew they were wrong.

                       ✑ WILSON MIZNER

How many of us catch ourselves taking our anger out on our husbands because we don't want to unload it on our babies? We won't scream at our baby, so we attack the most convenient target.

We know we're wrong, and we need to make amends. Being righteous only perpetuates a hurtful and reactionary pattern. Admitting our mistakes, on the other hand, empowers us. When we take responsibility for our actions and forgive ourselves for our mistakes, we will feel more loving toward ourselves and others. This will make it more possible to change our behavior and be more careful about our misdirected anger.

Making amends is one of the most loving things I can do for myself and for those I love.

I give myself, sometimes, admirable advice, but I am incapable of taking it.

☜ MARY WORTLEY MONTAGU

S ounds familiar, doesn't it? Giving advice to others about their childrearing problems is always easier than dealing with our own. When others come to us, we instantly turn into creative problem-solvers. Sometimes the wisdom that leaps from our lips astounds even us. But, when it comes to applying it to our own lives, we're always too busy or too tired or we make excuses like "it probably won't work with my baby."

I should listen more carefully to what I say to others; perhaps it's the advice I need to hear.

Self-Affirmation

At night, when the house is quiet and the children have all gone to sleep, I take a deep breath and listen to the steady beat of my heart.

✎ JILLIAN KLARL

*W*e all have had days when we are so thoroughly exhausted that we forget we exist. We feel numb and robotic, disconnected from ourselves and from the world. We stare at our face in the mirror and don't recognize who we see. Our insides are hollow, our energy is spent. We stare at a book, the T.V., yet absorb nothing. We are too tired to know we need to sleep. We vaguely wonder if we are living or merely existing from chore to chore.

Thankfully, the brag of our heart, the steady pulse of life, is there to remind us *we are alive*. Proudly, it beats, "I am, I am, I am." It calls us inside to the serenity of its motion and once there, we can be at peace.

The beat of my heart is my declaration of life.

The supreme happiness of life is the conviction of being loved for yourself, or, more correctly, being loved in spite of yourself.

         ❧ VICTOR HUGO

*O*ne of the greatest tests—and greatest victories—of motherhood is learning to love unconditionally. Not placing limitations on our love doesn't mean that we accept everything our children do. It does mean that we continue to demonstrate our love for them despite what they do. And they do test us—and our love—over and over.

By separating who our children are from what they do, we illustrate to them that they are not their actions. Just because they have done something dangerous or bad doesn't mean that they are dangerous or bad. By applying this simple wisdom we bolster our children's self-esteem.

When I love my child unconditionally, I show him that I love him even when I do not like his behavior—and this helps him to trust in my love.

*I have an intense desire to return to the womb.
Anybody's.*

WOODY ALLEN

No matter how strong and independent we are, we still need to be nurtured. The level of commitment and constant attention required for raising a child can tax us considerably. We give and give and give. There are days when we're just plain tired of being responsible. *We* want to be pampered and babied. *We* want to be tucked into bed with a bedtime story.

When we feel like we want to trade places with our baby, it's time to do something special for ourselves. Maybe for a day or two we could nurture ourselves, right in our own home by creating a womb of sorts. Let Dad take the children out to play, and while they're gone, we can hug our teddy bear and suck our thumb when no one's looking!

Sometimes nurturing myself means creating a space and place where I can be alone and responsible for no one but myself.

*Knowledge of what is possible is the beginning of
happiness.*

🐛 GEORGE SANTAYANA

*W*hy is it that women feel obligated to drop
whatever we're doing whenever someone
calls? We feel compelled to answer the door or pick
up the phone, when it rings, no matter how busy we
are.

Then, we have a baby, and necessity dictates that
we start recognizing our limitations. After a couple
times of answering the doorbell only to discover a
salesman with a useless product, we learn to peek out
the window. We buy an answering machine and
screen our calls. We figure out that we don't have to
entertain friends and relatives as soon as we arrive
home from the hospital. Maybe we're nursing the
baby, changing diapers, trying to take a nap, or simply
recovering from childbirth. When we realize these are
all legitimate reasons, we can set boundaries that are
appropriate for us.

**Managing my life as a new mother means I must
put myself and my child first.**

We can't form our children on our own concepts; we must take them and love them as God gives them to us.
     ❧ HERMANN AND DOROTHEA

*B*efore our baby is born we fantasize about who he will be and what he'll look like. We make elaborate plans for his life. Then he arrives and he's not at all like we expected. We thought he'd be blond, he's brunette. We thought he'd be a girl, he's a boy!

Babies do not come pre-packaged; they come as they are. Of course, it is only natural to have days when we wish they were different. Perhaps we wish our infant was calmer or more active. We wish he would sleep more and cry less. Then, when we really think about it, we realize that we can have as many expectations as we want, we just can't expect all of them to be actualized.

My child is not a piece of clay that I can mold to my likes and dislikes; he is his own person and he is a person I love.

He was teaching me something about flow,
about choosing the right moment for everything,
about enjoying the present.

🖜 ROBYN DAVIDSON

The mystics have always said that time is an illusion. Physicists have confirmed this fact.

Children innately know it. That is why they follow their own inner rhythms and flow of time. When we attempt to speed them up or slow them down, they usually resist. It's not that they're being stubborn, they're just responding to something that feels unnatural.

Like the rest of us, they will learn how to incorporate the artificial constraints of time. Hopefully, they will maintain their connection to a deeper knowing: that linear time is an illusion.

Children understand "flow." The child within me still remembers.

God only knows, and she ain't tellin'.

                   PAUL A. WILSON

*M*y father used to say this to me whenever I'd ask an impatient question like, "How long will it take them to fix the car so we can get to Grammie's house?"

Now that I'm a mother, I find I'm still asking questions that don't have an immediate answer. "How long do you think the baby will be sick?" "Do you think he'll be walking by his first birthday?"

As mothers, we feel we should know the answers to these questions, but we don't. Accepting the fact that we *can't know* helps us remember that life is untidy and full of uncertainties. We can't always plan it the way we'd like. When we respect this fact, we can stop trying to control the variables and start responding to whatever arises.

When I *react* to life's uncertainties, I am trying to control them. Maybe I could *respond* to them instead?

*If they could figure out a way to channel my anger,
they could solve the energy crisis.*

❧ WOODY ALLEN

We get so stressed out by the demands of motherhood that we end up angry about everything all the time. We lose our sense of humor and blow everything out of proportion. We're caught on a roller coaster of frustrated anger and we can't get off.

When we're in this state, we can't calm ourselves without some form of release. All our stress and tension has lodged itself in our bodies and we need to break the cycle of agitation by moving our anger out. Swimming is great. We can also strangle a pillow. Or, perhaps, we'd feel better if we wrote a nasty letter to no one in particular. Or we could follow Bette Midler's example and turn our anger into saucy humor. Who knows, we just might come up with something that makes us laugh at ourselves!

Feeling perpetually angry is no fun. Inventing new ways to release it is.

They gave each other a smile with a future in it.
                🖎 RING LARDNER

*F*or months, infants strive to master their facial muscles. Other than uncontrollable twitches and quirky squints, their faces remain expressionless. They use their eyes to communicate with us.

Then, one day, it happens. A gorgeous smile appears. It's no mistake, our baby is smiling at us. Somewhere inside, this little being has noticed our love and tenderness. Our corny jokes and philosophical conversations were heard. Our caresses gave sensual pleasure, and our funny faces delighted. Our hearts melt when we feel we are loved back.

It's not enough to know I am loved. I must feel it.

"Response-Ability"

The only way round is through.

🎋 ROBERT FROST

*T*here are no short cuts for a responsive parent. We must consider our children's feelings as equal to ours and always take their needs into account. We must be sensitive to their fears and respect their limitations.

Certainly, being a responsive parent is challenging and difficult. We may find ourselves pulling our hair out a bit more than the average parent simply because we are going that extra mile. When we incorporate our children's natural rhythms into our lives instead of expecting them to accommodate ours, it may mean not getting our way, or doing all the things we want to do—at least not at the present time.

Yet, to be actively involved with our children brings a great many rewards. We intimately know who they are and how they are.

Having the ability to respond is one of my strong points. If I go round instead of through, think of all I will have missed. . . .

Worry

Worry is like a rocking chair—it gives you something to do but it doesn't get you anywhere.

             ❧ DOROTHY GALYEAN

*A*ll mothers worry. We worry that our child isn't eating properly. We worry about our stress—is it affecting our child? Is he getting enough sleep?

If we can't find anything in our present situation to fuss about, there's always the future. Should I take this trip? What if it disrupts his sleeping pattern? What if he pokes other children in the eye? What if we run out of money? What if he ends up in jail as a drug dealer? We're consumed by things that are usually beyond our control. The more we worry, the more we lose sight of what is and become consumed by fictional events that rarely come to pass. Sure, worry gives us something to do, but it rarely gets us anywhere.

Worrying inhibits my ability to be in the present. Maybe I should be worrying about that!

The child whom many fathers share hath seldom known a father's care.

🐚 JOHN GAY

Women usually have more experience than men in caring for babies. We learned the basics babysitting, caring for a younger sibling or playing with our dolls. Most men never had these early experiences and when baby arrives, they're totally in the dark.

The steady demands of a newborn keep mothers busy. We assume leadership for our infant's care and everyone else is support staff. When our husbands look to us for guidance, we become impatient and irritable. It suddenly feels as if we have two children.

If we afford our husbands the same respect we expect when we're first learning something new, we'll benefit in the long run. In time, Dad can assume a greater portion of the responsibility because he's no longer "in training." And we get to relax a bit because we're no longer fully in charge. Could it be that our ship will run more smoothly with two captains at the helm?

Being the only "semi-expert" can be an added frustration. It helps to remember that my husband, just like my child, needs time to learn.

Well, we start out in our lives as little children, full of light and the clearest vision.

BRENDA UELAND

We all know what it's like to have "the clearest vision." Our dreams and inspirations flicker within us like an eternal flame. Yet when we focus solely on the needs of others, we lose sight of those things which lie deep inside of us. We feel cut off from the spiritual pulse of life and the heart of our creativity.

Children's vision is clear and unaltered by layers of perceptions. There is a directness and honesty in their interactions with the world. Their hearts are open, their eyes unflinching. Like our children, we still possess the lucid vision bestowed on us at birth, even if it feels like a vague memory. When it makes an appearance, we need to acknowledge its arrival by stopping whatever it is we're doing at that moment. Because if we convince ourselves we're too busy and ignore it, this exquisite second is lost, superseded by mundane details.

Vision is a gift of the soul. It illumines my place in the universe.

When wives and children and their sires are one,
'Tis like the harp and lute in unison.

꧁ CONFUCIUS

*E*ver notice how contented infants are when
mommy and daddy are together with them?
Children need what each parent has to offer. They
need to nurture their bond with daddy as much as
with mommy. They need a sense of unity and family
to encircle them.

For parents, the stress of merely *being parents* can
create separation and discord. Parents need to nurture
the harmony between them. They need to till the
soil of their common ground in order to make it rich
and fertile for their children. Otherwise, instead of
finding security in a harmonious family, children
withdraw from the screeching sounds of discord.

**To play an instrument requires patience and dedi-
cation. The harmony of my relationships takes the
same kind of loving commitment.**

Some of my best ideas come to me while I'm nursing my baby.

☞ JOYCE WILLAFORD

Nursing is a meditative activity. No matter how rushed or busy we are, we have to slow down. We have to be still. Our bodies know this. That is why our glands release certain hormones that help us to relax.

At first, some of us fight this process. We feel that nursing restricts us. We feel our time is wasted, and we see ourselves as unproductive. Yet, if we can learn to quiet our minds and calm our bodies, we will find that the time spent nursing is anything but wasted. The tranquility will help to replenish our strength. Like any meditative activity, nursing helps our creative and inspirational juices flow. The endless chatter of the mind quiets, making room for our best ideas to emerge.

Nursing benefits my child. Isn't it wonderful that it also benefits me?

Trouble is part of your life, and if you don't share it, you don't give the person who loves you a chance to love you enough.

             🪱 DINAH SHORE

*T*rouble is part of everyone's life. When we share it with those we trust, our troubles dissipate and, sometimes, even vanish. If our pain is heard, it can begin to dissolve.

When we keep our loved ones at a distance, we may think we are protecting *them*, when actually we are protecting ourselves. Afraid of being perceived as weak, we don't allow ourselves to be vulnerable. By excluding those we love from the troubled parts of our life, we don't give them the "chance to love us enough."

As Henry J. Kaiser once said, "Trouble is only opportunity in work clothes." Let's use the opportunity.

We are all in this together—by ourselves.

                       ❧ LILY TOMLIN

*M*others share an unspoken convenant. We draw strength from one another. We learn from each other. We make some of the same mistakes and revel in one another's successes. The common bond of motherhood gives us strength, it unites us and it gives us a sense of being "all in this together."

Yet, when we leave the circle of our friends and return home, a strange paradox becomes evident. Our life is still our life. Ultimately, the decisions we make belong to us, alone. Whether we allow others to influence our choices or occasionally make them for us, we must live with the outcome. No one else can live our life for us.

We *are* all in this together. We need the support of our community *and* we must rely on ourselves.

*I am years gone from my family and miles away...
but they raid by telephone with jarring suddenness;
they have the cyclic constancy of a mortgage; and they
are inevitable and relentless, like the erosion of my
remaining youth. Like certain frightening dreams, my
family returns.*

🍼 JERROLD MUNDIS

Whether we like it or not, family ties run deep.
There is something tangible and durable
about the bond we share with our parents and sib-
lings, regardless of whether we get along with or like
them. At no time is this more evident than when we
have a baby.

As a new mother, we get more attention from the
family than we've gotten in years. Relatives call more
frequently and they ask more personal questions.
They want to be a part of our child's lives. They want
to remind us that we are still a part of theirs.

**When the novelty of my new baby wears off, family
members will resume normal levels of attention
and involvement.**

Exuberance is beauty.

                         WILLIAM BLAKE

*B*abies are beautiful in their exuberance. They thrive in new environments because each new discovery is cause for delight. To them, life is rich and fresh, and they invite the new with vivacious eagerness.

How long has it been since we've felt this way? Have we allowed our routines to whittle away at our ability to be excited by new things? Have we told ourselves that we don't need a break because "things are just fine"? Have we neglected ourselves because we "can't spend money on frivolous things"?

Moms need vacations. We occasionally need to cut loose from our moorings and exercise our wings. We needn't hop on a plane to escape the trappings of the familiar, yet we need to experience the new. And, hopefully, like our children, we will shriek again with delight!

Imagining a vacation is one way to take a trip. But actual travel stirs the blood and puts real enthusiasm back in my life.

Nothing has a stronger influence psychologically on their environment, and especially on their children, than the unlived life of the parents.

C.G. JUNG

ne way to 'pour ourselves into our children' is to shower them with love and attention. Another way is to direct our unfulfilled dreams toward them, projecting who we always wanted to be onto them. We pour our energy into them, forgetting that their wee bodies cannot contain the enormity of our dreams. Our role as mothers is to be midwives to their discovery, so they may achieve *their own* dreams.

If I pour myself into my children, they will be filled with me, not themselves.

Wonder

If a child is to keep his inborn sense of wonder. . . he needs the companionship of at least one adult who can share it, rediscovering with him the joy, excitement and mystery of the world we live in.

RACHEL CARSON

*I*n the children's story, *The Little Prince,* adults are portrayed as wooden and unimaginative people who are continually misinterpreting what children say. They cannot see the world as the children see it: full of mystery and magic.

Mothers can nurture a child's inborn sense of wonder and enchantment. We can help them to "rediscover the joy, excitement and mystery of the world we live in," especially when we keep it alive within ourselves. Like the little prince, we can see the elephant the snake has swallowed instead of declaring that it is impossible for a snake to swallow an elephant. We can wish on falling stars, find secret messages in the sand and hear tiny voices whispering in the swaying wheat fields.

Living is a gift of wonder. Let me share it with my child.

I felt protective of her because she was so fragile, and I was afraid I might lose her. Until Emily was three years old, I never felt certain that she would be all right.

🐛 KAY ANDERSON SAAVEDRA

Those of us who deliver a baby prematurely often feel anxious about our child's survival. She has had so many brushes with death in her early months that we try not to get our hopes up. Yet hope is all we have.

For the first few years, we feel protective. We desperately want to believe she'll be all right and yet, we catch ourselves watching her closely, searching for any indications that might tell us otherwise. We want to ensure her continued existence, all the while knowing that to do so is beyond our capabilities.

Although a part of us may continue to feel uncertain, we eventually relax in the knowing that our child has taken hold of life. She is here to stay.

Life is precious. I will never forget just how precious it is.

Trespass not on his solitude.

             ❧ RALPH WALDO EMERSON

*I*nfants need solitude. They need time away from the tremendous amount of stimulation they encounter once outside the womb. Placing them in their crib to play alone or on a blanket in a quiet room works wonders.

In a few short months, our children will take the initiative. They will tell us in their own non-verbal way that they want to be left alone more frequently. They will fuss when we don't respect their sacred space. This move toward independence can be threatening to us, and causes most of us to unknowingly interfere in our child's secret play. Maybe we fear imminent separation? When we see that their wanting to be alone doesn't mean they're rejecting us, we can appreciate and respect their need for solitude.

Infants need to reflect on their inner world as much as parents do. Maybe I could practice being alone together with my child.

What the mother sings to the cradle goes all the way to the coffin.

🖎 HENRY WARD BEECHER

I'm always surprised by adults who think babies can't understand what we're saying just because they're pre-verbal. What a grave mistake. By three months old, an infant can communicate with different cries and facial expressions. At six months old, babies can recognize familiar objects. Even when infants can't understand our words, they can certainly sense the feelings behind them. They're tuned in to the tone of our voice, and understand that different tones mean different things. Compliments and encouragement make their little faces beam. Clapping our hands and imitating their sounds leaves them overjoyed. We are important to them. So important that what we say stays with them.

Never underestimate the power of words. They can elevate the spirit or wound the soul.

What do they think my uterus is—a tracking device?
❧ ROSEANNE ARNOLD

hy is it that women always know where everything is? It can only be the result of a sex-linked gene. Otherwise, why would we bother to clutter our minds with the whereabouts of missing socks and underwear, letters and ketchup bottles?

While we are proud to have such an impeccable memory, it can be a drag to be the household "tracking device." Once our talent is discovered, everyone depends on mom to know where everything is. When we ask them where they think they might have left their belongings, a pained expression comes over their faces. How could we ask such a cruel question? They'd rather have their teeth extracted one by one than to exercise a skill that is already so highly developed in their own mother.

James Thurber once complained, "I hate women because they always know where things are." But it's convenient, isn't it, James?

*People are subject to moods, to temptations and fears,
lethargy and aberration and ignorance, and the
staunchest qualities shift under the stresses and
strains of daily life. Like liberty, they are not secured
for all time. They are not inevitable.*

ILKA CHASE

We all carry an image in our heads of who we
are and how we should be. But these standards are ideals. We look to the exceptional times in
our lives as examples of how we should be every
single day. We forget that we're only human, after all.

Life changes, and we with it. We do not attain an
ideal state of existence and live that way indefinitely.
Our qualities and our values are subject to change,
especially under the stresses and strains of bringing
up children. Some days we flourish, other days our
children bring out the worst in us. When we can own
and accept that *all these qualities* belong to us, then
we can be more honest about our image of ourselves.

**To err is human. . . . When I am no longer human, I
cease to exist.**

*Despite the joyful gains of motherhood, there is
something that is lost—a sense of self maybe, or living
for yourself. Part of what I missed was the acceptance,
approval and self-esteem that comes from pursuing a
career.*

🕮 LESLIE GEORGE

Motherhood often feels like a thankless job.
Much of what we do is invisible and cannot
be measured quantitatively. Therefore, we tend to
discount the enormous effort it takes to raise
children.

Work, on the other hand, has concrete signs of
progress. Our hard work is rewarded—with kudos,
raises, promotions. Not only that, but projects come
to a completion. We see the fruits of our labor in
tangible results. If our child is happy and can read, it
is not necessarily because of us. Sure, we can take
credit or be given credit, but it's always tenuous
credit, and this can affect our self-esteem. That is why
it is essential for mothers to look to themselves for
definition and approval instead of waiting for acco-
lades from others.

**Raising my children is a labor of love. Like a rare
gem, its worth cannot be calculated.**

If it weren't for pickpockets, I'd have no sex life at all.
❧ RODNEY DANGERFIELD

Having a baby can significantly diminish our chances for successful lovemaking. Between hormonal mood swings, postpartum dryness, and just plain exhaustion, we're lucky to have a sex life at all.

Like Rodney Dangerfield, we must maintain some levity about our situation. Otherwise sex, like so many other things in our lives, becomes a pressure, not an enjoyment. Be creative. Cuddle and laugh while watching old movies. Check into a hotel. Dance cheek-to-cheek in the living room. Light candles and take a hot bath together. Remember that sex isn't limited to the bedroom.

"Things not being the way they used to" could be more fun than "things being the way they used to."

*A sound marriage is not based on complete frankness;
it is based on sensible reticence.*

❧ MORRIS L. ERNST

*H*onesty doesn't mean blurting out whatever
we think and feel whenever we think and
feel it. When we're in the midst of postpartum
depression, our words can hurt. Granted, the postpartum period is a time when we're least able to exercise "sensible reticence." However, we need to be
sensitive to others, because much of what we say we
don't really mean. Simply explaining this in advance
to our loved ones will help them better understand
those moments when our "complete frankness" is
hurtful.

Although we cannot always control what comes
out of our mouths, and often can't recall what we've
said, we need to sort out and communicate what our
real complaints and frustrations are.

**During the postpartum period everything is in a
state of flux. Being aware and doing the best I can
may be the best I can do.**

Single Mothers

I demand for the unmarried mother, as a sacred channel of life, the same reverence and respect as for the married mother; for Maternity is a cosmic thing and once it has come to pass, our conventions must not be permitted to blaspheme it.

✍ BEN LINDSEY

*I*n the not-so-distant past, unwed mothers were viewed as outcasts. Fortunately, attitudes have changed and we have more freedom. Today, some women are choosing to either have and/or raise their children by themselves, preferring to be single or to live in a communal setting. Other women, abandoned by their male partners and left to raise their children alone, are not subjected to the same degree of societal disdain as they once would have been. Motherhood is being given the respect it deserves and marriage is no longer the determining factor. Finally, we have come to recognize that "Maternity is a cosmic thing."

A mother is a mother is a mother. Married or not, our commitment to our children is still as deep, and our gifts are still as sweet.

The time to relax is when you don't have time for it.
              ❧ SYDNEY J. HARRIS

ime is seen as a scarce commodity, yet we
rarely take the time to enjoy it. The busier we
get, the more we take on. It's a vicious cycle, and our
lives spiral out of control. We become overwrought
with nervous exhaustion. When we're in this
state, it's actually painful to relax because the minute
we do, we feel the tension and strain in our mind
and muscles. So, we drink coffee, eat sugar, or listen
to raucous music in order to sustain our hyperactivity.
We make excuses for why we can't relax—we don't
have the time!

Eventually, we may see how destructive this pattern
is to ourselves and others. When we recognize how
much it disrupts communication, intimacy, and peace
of mind, we stop making excuses and we start making
time to relax.

**It isn't easy to step off of a runaway train, unless I
remember that I'm the conductor.**

Fear

If a man (or woman) harbors any sort of fear, it percolates through all his thinking, damages his personality, makes him landlord to a ghost.

LLOYD DOUGLAS

Fear of a child's death is universal. We all have rushes of crippling panic, dark scenarios about what might happen to our children.

Those of us who have recently become mothers are particularly prone to these fears. For the first time, we are confronted with our profound vulnerability and the responsibility of protecting someone besides ourselves. We may go on for months with these grotesque phantoms invading our thoughts and dreams. If we allow them to, they can consume us. However, if we confront our fears, it helps us develop a second sense which lets us know when our child's life is in real peril. And, like a lioness, we can fiercely protect our cubs.

I want to be like the lioness: at peace with my child, yet alert to real danger.

*That is the happiest conversation where there is no
competition, no vanity, but a calm quiet interchange
of sentiments.*

🖎 SAMUEL JOHNSON

*I*sn't it nice to telephone a friend after baby goes
to sleep and all is quiet in the house? Talking
about our new experiences helps us to unwind. As
our words flow, our tension flows out with them.
Unhurried, we share each other's lives. Talking to a
close friend is as soothing as balm. We know someone cares about us. There is no competition, no pre-
tense, only the calm quiet interchange of feelings.

**Talking to a close friend reminds me of the
true value of friendship. Let me be thankful for
the ease of our conversations.**

I feel bad that I don't feel worse.

🐛 MICHAEL FRAYN

 sk any mother and she will say the same thing. Leaving Baby with Dad while she escapes from the house feels great!

Yes, we try to drum up sympathy for poor ol' Dad, home all alone with baby. But, somehow, we just don't get very far. Even the uneasy smile we see come over Dad's face as we walk out the door doesn't stop us from leaving. While we'd like to stay and help out....

It's our turn! Finally, it's our turn! For a few luscious hours we get to experience life without baby. We almost feel bad that we don't feel worse—almost.

Freedom, sweet freedom. A taste of it is all I need.

Listening is not merely not talking, though even that is beyond most of our powers; it means taking a vigorous, human interest in what is being told us. You can listen like a blank wall or like a splendid auditorium where every sound comes back fuller and richer.

        ❧ ALICE DUER MILLER

*L*istening is not simply hearing. It requires our attention and response. Not only do we absorb what another person is saying, we absorb the person himself. Listening gives us entrance into another's world and we have the opportunity to see and experience the world through his eyes. When we respond, if we've truly listened, "every sound comes back fuller and richer."

As mothers, we listen not only with our ears, we listen with our whole being. That is how we know when our baby is ill or doesn't like someone. By watching his eyes, we know what he is communicating. And, when we respond, our baby knows he is heard.

Listening is an art. My baby helps me to fine-tune my talents.

A committee of one gets things done.

🖎 JOE RYAN

others often find themselves in difficult negotiating positions. We try to reach a consensus on what is best for our child, yet we run into obstacles that weigh us down. For some of us, that obstacle is our husband. His reluctance to try anything new can prevent us from moving forward.

If we want a unanimous decision from the "parental committee," we have two options. We can wait until our husbands are convinced of the validity of our actions, or we can wait until they come up with a viable solution. Either way, our momentum is stalled. Fortunately, there is another option. We can feel confident that the situation calls for a unilateral decision, and trust in our own expertise. We can be a "committee of one" and hope we're right.

Difficult decisions are more difficult when I don't have support and cooperation. I may have to trust my own judgment.

Children, like animals, use all their senses to discover the world. Then artists come along and discover it the same way all over again.

           🌿 EUDORA WELTY

*B*abies are like dolphins. They have heightened sensitivity to the world around them. They touch whatever they come into contact with. They absorb every sound and sight. They not only hear the wind and waves, they experience them through every pore in their body. They are one with creation.

How long has it been since we've felt this way? Do our senses feel worn and dull? Do we feel like strangers to the earth? Do our lives feel void of sensual nourishment? Whenever we go too long without experiencing oneness with nature, we feel alienated. We feel outside the flow of life. Maybe, like the artist, we need to discover the world all over again with all our senses.

Children are sensual creatures, and so are their mothers. Let me open my senses to life and be fed.

Beauty

Ask a toad what is beauty? . . . a female with two great round eyes coming out of her little head, a large flat mouth, a yellow belly and a brown back.

♫ VOLTAIRE

*E*very mother thinks her baby is beautiful. And all babies are beautiful regardless of their physical appearance. It doesn't matter whether our infant's ears stick out or her nose is big. Mothers can see the radiance of their newborn; the radiance of a new life. And that life has come from inside of us; it is the most beautiful part of us.

Yes, babies are beautiful. They teach us to see beyond appearances, straight into the mystery of life. And there is nothing more beautiful than that.

When the beauty within shines outward, it is radiance. And my baby shines radiantly!

Forget your mistakes, but remember what they taught you.

🖐 DOROTHY GALYEAN

Sometimes we have a tendency to personalize mistakes. We chastise ourselves by keeping a tally and view our mistakes as transgressions rather than simple blunders.

We must remember that mistakes are often opportunities for learning. And, sometimes, the higher the tuition, the greater the lesson. While we should "forget our mistakes," we must not forget what they have taught us. Otherwise, our hard-earned wisdom will be of no use.

Learning from my mistakes builds character. And, from the looks of it, I'm quite a colorful character!

As I repeatedly heard career women in this study say,
"What I really need is a wife." But maybe they don't
need "wives"; maybe they need careers basically
redesigned to suit workers who also care for families.
This redesign would be nothing short of a
revolution. . . .

            ARLIE HOCHSCHILD

*H*ow many of us have said at some time: "I
need a wife"?

Those of us who divide our time between home
and the workplace often feel overwhelmed. When we
"punch out" at work, we "punch in" at home, and
start "the second shift." Unlike our energy supply,
work is endless. We have little time or emotional
energy for those we love. We burn out.

Unless working conditions change drastically, we
will continue to burn out. The chasm between work
and family life will continue to widen. If our careers
and our husbands' are not "redesigned to suit workers who also care for families," this chasm will tear us
apart. It will leave our children wanting.

As Sojourner Truth once said: "If de fust woman
God ever made was strong enough to turn the
world upside down all alone, dese women toged-
der ought to be able to turn it back, and get it right
side up again!"

When you are a mother, you are never really alone in your thoughts.... A mother always has to think twice, once for herself and once for her child.

           ❧ SOPHIA LOREN

*A*t first, "never really being alone" may feel like an invasion. Our thoughts feel crowded, as another being so fully occupies our lives. It is difficult to focus. We are easily distracted. Even when our thoughts stray, they eventually circle back to our child.

Like our stomachs stretched during pregnancy, our minds now stretch to accommodate our child. We must expand ourselves to encompass a life that is so closely connected to ours. In time, we will be able to hold our own thoughts while thoughts of our child hover in the wings.

By the ninth month, I didn't think I could hold my child inside of me any longer. Now, I must expand my mind.

We are raised to believe that mother love is different from other kinds of love. It is not open to error, doubt, or to the ambivalence of ordinary affections. This is an illusion. Mothers may love children, but they sometimes do not like them. The same woman who may be willing to put her body between her child and a runaway truck will often resent the day by day sacrifice the child unknowingly demands of her time, sexuality and self-development.

🤚 NANCY FRIDAY

Nancy Friday has captured one of the great paradoxes of motherhood. While maternal love *is* different than other kinds of love, it is still susceptible to feelings of doubt, resentment, and "the ambivalence of ordinary affections." And why not?

Unknowingly, our children place tremendous demands on us. Although the sacrifices are not without reward, we may need to ask for help from others. Otherwise, we'll resent the demands, and miss the gratifications motherhood has to offer.

Sacrifice is an inescapable fact of motherhood. Fortunately, it is not the only fact of motherhood.

The suspense is terrible. I hope it will last.

                    OSCAR WILDE

*D*uring pregnancy, there's a heightened anticipation that is intoxicating. We examine our bodies daily, hunting for the signs that substantiate our rather queasy state. We want to know about this little person who is inside of us. What will he look like? What will the birth be like? We hope the suspense will last. That is, until our ninth month, when we realize that our body is not going to reabsorb this child and we must give birth or explode.

After the birth, we are again filled with suspense. So many surprises lie ahead and we await them with gleeful expectancy. We wonder when our baby will roll over, get a full head of hair, and produce his first tooth.

With the advent of motherhood, we gain a heightened awareness of the cycles and flow of life's rhythms. We learn to be open to change, growth, and unpredictability. And we are filled with anticipation because we can never be sure what will come next.

May my life always be filled with suspense!

I have had enough.

        ❧GOLDA MEIR

*M*others need to set limits. If we don't, we'll find ourselves stretched to the limit! However, many of us push ourselves until we have no choice but to drop everything and scream "I've had enough." We confuse those around us because we tell them everything is fine, then suddenly, we explode.

Some of us take the passive-aggressive approach. We hide our feelings, as we make life miserable for the other members of the family. But our hostile actions say, we've had enough.

It is important to learn to recognize these signals that warn us we are approaching our limits. Whenever we feel impatient with our kids, it's a sign. Whenever we grumble under our breath as we pick up toys and dirty dishes, it's a sign. As we come to recognize the signs, we will go over the edge less and less.

Everyone has limits. It is a strength to know mine.

Love is an ocean of emotions entirely surrounded by expenses.

🖙 LORD DEWAR

*O*nce we have a baby, we are shocked by the amount of money it takes to raise him. The cost of clothing, toys, diapers, furniture, and visits to the doctor adds up quickly. Many of us have to work just to make ends meet. Possibly, for the first time in our lives, we must budget our money or borrow from others. We wonder whether we can adequately support those we love, when we feel we're drowning in expenses.

Having to worry about every dollar we spend isn't fun. Fortunately, we are resourceful. We can borrow clothes or shop at "next-to-new" clothing stores. And sometimes, we can simply do without. Our babies don't need the best of everything, they need the best of us—which they're not going to get if we're stressed out over money.

Financial stress is real. However, being obsessed with money leaves me little energy for those I love.

. . . In the early days of parenting, we keep our pain and confusion to ourselves, fearing that confiding in others will confirm our fears of our own inadequacy.
🦢 PEGGY O'MARA

*T*he first year of our child's life is often the most difficult. Parenting is more complex than we ever imagined: We didn't expect so many sleepless nights; we didn't know a baby could cry so much or for so long. The things that used to work don't work anymore, and we find ourselves doubting our own abilities as mothers.

During these times, it is important to confide in others who share our experience. Yet it is just these times when we keep our pain to ourselves. We don't want anyone to think we're not a good mother, so we withdraw and suffer alone.

Even if we're afraid, we must reach out for advice and support. Instead of being judged, we will probably find others who share the very same insecurities.

Confiding in others is not publicizing my weaknesses. It is a way to get the reassurance I need to be a more confident parent.

Flowers grow out of dark moments.

          ❧ CORITA KENT

Some of our children experienced difficult births: complicated deliveries; emergency c-sections; premature births. Their entrance into the world was all but serene. What began as a euphoric occasion for us turned into a nightmare of dashed hopes, fear, and failed dreams. Never have we felt so vulnerable and alone. No one, not even those closest to us, could change what was happening. We felt helpless, and we had no choice but to trust in others to safely bring our baby into the world. Love was all we could offer and it didn't feel like it was enough.

Luckily, for the majority of us, things turned out all right. Instead of dwelling on what we were physically unable to do, we were able to see what we did do. Our love and trust were all we had to offer and they were enough.

Love is the one constant I can depend on. It will see me through the difficult times.

*I knew I was an unwanted baby when I saw that my
bath toys were a toaster and a radio.*

🖐 JOAN RIVERS

Some of us felt that our parents were trying
to get rid of us. Now that we are parents, we
realize that that's exactly what our parents were
trying to do!

Parents need time to themselves. We need to get
reacquainted and nurture the bond that brought
us together in the first place. We want to talk without
interruptions, to catch up on each others' lives.
And we can't do that at bedtime when we're too
exhausted to talk—or to listen. We need to spend the
night out and pretend we don't have children, just so
we can remember what the other person is like.

Yes, our parents needed time to themselves, and so
do we. Hopefully, we'll be able to explain this to our
children without making them feel excluded. Maybe
they can see it as getting rid of *us* for the evening!

**Parenthood doesn't mean my husband and I always
have to hang out in crowds.**

*Having children is like having a bowling alley
installed in your brain.*

           ✎ MARTIN MULL

*M*otherhood places constant demands on our attention. Endless interruptions, annoying distractions, and erratic demands make it impossible to think straight. We can't remember what we were thinking or doing before someone or something started to clamor for our attention. We are juggling bowling balls and we never know when the pins are going to fall.

Happily, a primary characteristic of motherhood is adaptability. Despite persistent interruptions, we learn to focus while being responsive. We sit in the eye of the hurricane, keeping our children under constant surveillance as they swirl around us. No longer do we expect to do anything from start to finish. Instead, we do a little here, a little there, until, at last, we've finished whatever it is we were doing.

If I don't learn how to concentrate amid the noise and interruptions, I'll end up feeling like a gutter ball. Flexibility will spare me this fate.

Learning how to be a mother is not a matter of adopting a certain set of attitudes, but of expressing one's own personality in the task of responding flexibly to the child's needs.

❧ SHEILA KITZINGER

*M*any of us have wanted children since we were young. We felt the desire to be a mother long before we were biologically capable. We named our make-believe sons and daughters, and with our imaginations, we filled in their eye color, skin tone, and the texture of their hair.

Some of us carefully arranged our lives, trying to put all the pieces in place before we had children. We planned and planned, waiting for the right time to conceive.

Then we became mothers and found that even with all of our planning, children do not fit neatly into our lives. We learned the hard way that being a mother "is not a matter of adopting a certain set of attitudes." We have to bring ourselves to the process moment by moment.

Just because I plan to be a certain way doesn't mean that's how I will turn out.

At work, you think of the children you have left at home. At home, you think of the work you've left unfinished. Such a struggle is unleashed within yourself. Your heart is rent.

          🖐 GOLDA MEIR

*W*hether we work out of necessity or because we want to, the dilemma is the same. We cannot possibly give one hundred percent to work *and* family. Although we do our best to juggle these two important aspects of our lives, it seems that one is always being sacrificed for the other. We wonder whether the daily grind will wear us down so that neither aspect of our life is fulfilling and we might have to choose between our family and our career.

Fortunately, for many of us, it is this creative stress that forces us to find a realistic solution. It forces us to get our priorities straight, and for this reason, we may find that we succeeded at work *because* of our children, not in spite of them.

Straddling two worlds is like riding two horses. If I can just head them both in the same direction, I won't be torn apart.

Those who lose dreaming are lost.

               AUSTRALIAN ABORIGINAL PROVERB

After the euphoria of childbirth wears off, most of us take a nose dive into the "baby blues." Our raised spirits drop below our knees as the reality of caring for a newborn sets in.

Struggling to meet the demands of each new day, we no longer have time to dream. The change is so sudden that it knocks us off-balance. At first, we wonder if it will always be this way. Then, we become afraid that it *will*. Will we ever dream again, and will our dreams be realized? We feel lost.

Over time, we see the transient nature of each phase of motherhood. Somewhere between the first three to six months, things ease up a bit. We learn to make time for our dreams. Some of us may even jot them down before they evaporate, returning to them later to glean their wisdom.

My dreams are not expendable. If I lose them, then I am truly lost.

My mother had a great deal of trouble with me but I think she enjoyed it.

&\ MARK TWAIN

*O*ur children can be adorable when they're mischievious, and it's sometimes difficult to keep a straight face when we have to discipline them. At other times, the trouble they get into can be exasperating. Yet, when they lunge forward to bite because their gums hurt, or take a swipe at us to see our reaction, we usually end up laughing. Most of us have to stifle our giggles after we say "no" or "don't" because children's response is so funny. They usually think our neophyte attempts at discipline are a silly new game.

Our children come armed with curiosity, determination, stamina, and a penchant for comic routines. Half the time, we enjoy the trouble they give us. However, we'd better not let them know it.

Getting into mischief is part of the fun of being a child. Watching my child get into mischief is part of the fun of being a parent.

*If a man does not keep pace with his companions,
perhaps it is because he hears a different drummer. Let
him step to the music he hears, however measured or
far away.*

🖎 HENRY DAVID THOREAU

*I*f asked, we would all say we believe in individuality. We want our child to know his own heart and mind. Yet as early as our child's first year of life, we compare him to others. We wonder why he isn't doing the same things other children his age are doing. And we worry.

Differences tend to make us uneasy until we finally become comfortable with the fact that our baby has his own likes and dislikes, and his own way of doing things. He does what most of us do: he follows the beat of his own drum.

**My child may not always exhibit the qualities of a
saint. But I'll love him just as he is.**

Accepting Sleeplessness

Every morning I woke up tired and angry until I realized that sleep, as I knew it, no longer existed. Now, I only wake up tired.

NANCY ISON

The erratic sleep patterns of a new born quickly turn mothers into irritable and grumpy grinches. On some mornings, our tempers are so bad that we make Genghis Khan look like a social worker. We want our sleep! And we want just as much of it as we've always had!

When we finally accept this unpleasant fact of motherhood, our outlook changes. We become masters of the "sneaky sleep." We learn to lean our head back on the couch while our baby is feeding and catch a quick snooze. We learn the value of naps—when baby goes down, we go down. We learn to forfeit an eight o'clock T.V. movie so we can get an extra two hours of sleep.

I can't always change my child's sleeping pattern, but I can change my attitude. Acceptance is the key.

Self-Reflection

My father was often angry when I was most like him.
ꙮ LILLIAN HELLMAN

Children look to us for a reflection of who they are. Yet children are also mirrors. They mirror who we are and how we are.

Ever notice how their mood changes whenever we become tense? Keen observers, they often sense our inner turmoil before we do. In fact, we may not be aware of what is going on inside of us until we see it acted out in our child's behavior.

What we see may not always be to our liking, since kids have an uncanny ability to mimic the traits we most dislike in ourselves. They bring our mannerisms, voice tones, nervous habits, and facial expressions to life. We see ourselves in living color. What better opportunity for growth?

My children are a reflection of me. They help me to see what I'd like to change as well as the aspects of myself I'd like to keep.

Spoiling

What's all this talk about spoiling a baby? I'm just giving them what they need and deserve!

           ✍ LINDA D'AGROSA

*U*ntil recently, most experts encouraged strict parenting. They warned against spoiling a baby. Although their recommendations went against most women's maternal instincts, they assured us that their theories were sound.

Today, more of us rely on our intuition and judgment. As a result, childrearing practices have changed dramatically. We realize that babies' actions reflect genuine needs rather than manipulative ploys. Usually, when we give them what they want, we are "just giving them what they need and deserve."

There's a difference between giving and giving in. In time, I will learn how to distinguish between the two.

Guilt: the gift that keeps on giving.

🎗 ERMA BOMBECK

*F*or mothers who choose to work, guilt is no stranger. Whether we love our work or hate it, there is a nagging feeling that we should be at home caring for our child. We know our absence affects our little one, and it pains us to think that it might affect her in adverse ways. Secretly, we want our child to be happy about our choice to work. We want her permission, and when we don't get it, we feel guilty. We wonder who should come first? And what does "coming first" mean? We question our ability to love and what being a good mother really means. We're guilt-ridden until we can reach a comfortable truce, and accept our choice to work.

Next time "the gift of guilt" is delivered to my door, I'm not going to sign for the package.

Being a mother is rewarding to one's female instincts, trying to one's nerves, physically exhausting, emotionally both frustrating and satisfying, and above all, not to be undertaken lightly.

               ❦ DR. MARGARET RAPHAEL

*R*arely are first time mothers confident and self-assured. More often than not, we're cautious and careful, nervous and neurotic. We prepare for the worst. To us first time moms, motherhood is not only "not to be undertaken lightly," it's a serious job where everything depends on us. We feel like the night watchman, always on guard. Is it any surprise we feel worn out?

Whether we attribute it to exhaustion or maturity, our fears recede and our confidence returns. Being serious about our mothering doesn't mean we must be humorless or controlling. When we feel comfortable enough, we might resign from the post of night watchman and join the others on the swings.

When I'm dead serious about my mothering, I feel dead tired.

People change and forget to tell each other.
LILLIAN HELLMAN

*W*hen we have a baby, we change. Frequently, the changes are so subtle and imperceptible that we can't adequately explain or describe them. All we know is that we're not the same, and this affects our relationships. Some friends slowly drift away. Other friends are more directly involved in our current life and we feel closer to them.

Lasting friendships are the ones that don't require us to verbalize all of our changes. Although we may choose to share our feelings about how we see ourselves changing, we don't *need* to in order to sustain a friendship. Our changes are understood and respected by our true friends. They are accepted as a natural part of our personal evolution as well as the evolution of the relationship.

Relationships fade and go through phases like the moon. My true friends endure through all my passages.

Anxiety is a thin stream of fear trickling through the mind. If encouraged, it cuts a channel into which all other thoughts are drained.

ARTHUR SOMERS ROCHE

et's face it, most of us new moms are anxious about almost everything. During the first few days of our newborn's life, we imagine the worse. We're sure we can't hear breathing over the monitor. We're convinced that our baby will smother under the covers. We're haunted by all the horrible stories other mothers have so generously shared. "It's only a matter of time before they all happen to *my* baby!"

When we fixate on our fear, it skews our perspective and we work ourselves up into a frenzy. We can't sleep, even though we're exhausted. We need to get a sanity check. We need to talk with someone we trust who can allay our fears and steady our nerves. It would help to compare notes with another new mom so we can find out that she's doing the same thing we are. Then, we can both have a much needed laugh!

Anxiety is fear that has taken the reins of my mind and run with them. It's time for me to take control of the reins.

O young thing, your mother's lovely armful!
How sweet the fragrance of your body.

✑ EURIPIDES

*B*abies inspire awe—so perfect is the smallness of their body, so pure and sweet their fragrance. They help us to remember the ineffable beauty of being human.

Their scent, like freshly-fallen snow or crisp midnight air, reminds us of what is good with the world. We see the perfection in life instead of focusing on its negative aspects. We witness the love in our babies' eyes, a love untainted by pain and hardship.

Even as our children grow older, these sweet, sweet scents return to us. They fill our senses. We pause and give thanks for this gift of innocence.

A baby's sweet fragrance stirs memories deep inside of me. I remember the perfection in new life and feel it in myself.

Test Without Answers

Everything has been figured out except how to live.

❖ JEAN-PAUL SARTRE

*L*ife is one big test. Sometimes we're prepared for its lessons, sometimes not. Motherhood is learning moment by moment; sometimes we know what we're doing, sometimes we wish we had instructions. Surely, something as important as this would come with directions!

Sometimes we imagine what it would be like to know everything in advance. Raising a child would be more like following a recipe than fumbling around in the dark. Life would be easier, more convenient. Life would be dull. We'd miss the unfolding drama, the spontaneity and suspense. We'd miss the unknown.

Luckily, life is not a multiple choice test. I don't have to be confined to one answer—that's what makes it so interesting!

Making the decision to have a child—it's momentous.
It is to decide forever to have your heart go walking
around outside your body.

ELIZABETH STONE

*P*regnancy is not always a planned or celebrated event. It may come at a tumultuous
time in our lives. We feel desperate as we grapple
with one of the most difficult dilemmas a woman can
face: "Do I want to have this baby?" We wonder if
we're prepared for parenthood—ready to provide the
emotional, psychological, physical, and financial
support a child needs.

Accepting and adjusting to an unanticipated
pregnancy can be a difficult process. We can't look
into the future and be sure everything will turn
out fine. There are no guarantees. We take a gamble
that will last for the rest of our lives.

Those of us who go through with this "accident"
may end up being surprised. A surprise is something
you didn't know you wanted until it happens.

Surprises come in many forms, and sometimes
seemingly unpleasant ones turn out to be
wonderful.

An actress' life is so transitory—suddenly you're a building.

            ❦ HELEN HAYES

A mother's life is not unlike that of an actress. Lifetimes fill minutes. We experience a multitude of emotions, and we undergo a variety of transformations throughout the course of each day. We step in and out of roles: cook, teacher, manager, coach, cheerleader, pupil, lover, and clown, and we must draw on our inner experience to fulfill each one. When we have no similar experiences to draw on, we improvise—"suddenly we're a building."

A talented actress does not lose herself in a variety of roles; rather, she brings herself to each of them. A talented mother does the same thing.

*The most important thing a father can do for his
children is to love their mother.*

              THEODORE HESBURGH

*F*amily unity is very important to children.
They need harmony and security. They sense
friction between their parents, and it makes them
uneasy. They fear that any turmoil might be their
fault.

This does not mean that we must hide our feelings.
Every couple feels the added strain of caring for an
infant. Every couple experiences anger and resentment. What is important is how we handle these
potentially volatile feelings. Do we wait until our
child is asleep before we enter into any heated discus-
sions? Or do we have a habit of blowing up in front
of him? Are our children witnesses to our arguments,
and not to our atonements?

**Just as we express our frustration and anger, so
must we express our love. That is how we
measure our success or failure at being parents.**

Beauty is an ecstasy; it is as simple as hunger. There is really nothing to be said about it.

                ❧W. SOMERSET MAUGHAM

*A*s women, we have the unique privilege of giving birth. The strenuous process is often likened to a marathon. Although we cannot see the path ahead, we must trust ourselves to move with every contraction. Rhythmically, we go inside ourselves, our thoughts are synchronized with our muscles. We concentrate hard, then harder, until we hold a focal point with our entire being. Every breath is the breath of life.

When we see the results of our labor, we are ecstatic. We're deeply moved by the tiny face that emerges from us. We are struck by the pure beauty; "it is as simple as hunger."

I have been witness to the beauty of creation. I am truly blessed.

Exhaustion

I said some words to the close and holy darkness and then I slept.

& DYLAN THOMAS

For mothers, those words are often: "God, help me make it through another day!"

Being a mother is an exhausting job and most nights we feel like zombies. Every day is so full that when we finally reach our bed, we say a quick prayer for our sanity, then pull the covers over our head.

Our brain is mush. Before we drop off to sleep, nervous exhaustion causes us to think of all the things we should have done. It's frustrating being this tired. We feel resentful. And, because we are so tired, we feel it would take too much energy to significantly change the situation. Under these circumstances, it's easy to have a "things will never change" attitude. Yet if we break down each project into smaller pieces, we will accomplish things. Instead of feeling that we merely survived each day, we'll feel a growing confidence that we can get things done, even if it's not as quickly as we would like.

I deserve a hand for whatever I am able to accomplish in a day, including a nap!

Resistance

*It is not true that life is one damn thing after another
... it's the same damn thing over and over.*
🐚 EDNA ST. VINCENT MILLAY

On the surface, a mother's life can give the
appearance of being "the same damn thing
over and over." Yet the everyday possibilities of
growth make life anything but repetitive. It is only
when we resist change and growth, that we stagnate.
The same problems do occur over and over.

Why do we resist? Because losing a "former self"
often feels like a death. We feel out of control and
want guarantees. Will the new me feel better? Will I
have a stronger sense of self?

Until we accept the process of change, we won't
feel like ourselves, we'll feel like someone we used
to be.

**Being consumed with the outcome of my growth
only creates more resistance. Maybe this time I can
trust the direction of my inner journey.**

The entry of a child into any situation changes the whole situation.

🐝 IRIS MURDOCH

*I*sn't it amazing to watch how people respond to the presence of a child?

When the child is a crying infant, others become tense and irritated. On airplanes, they move to another seat. Yet when a child is contented and interactive, people soften. A gentler, more vulnerable side is revealed. Children's natural ability to be themselves allows others to be more fully who they are.

Yes, children add a new dimension to any situation. What that dimension will be depends on the mood of the child and the mood of the adult.

A child has a profound impact on everyone around him. Being oneself will do that.

Self-Esteem

To be told we are loved is not enough. We must feel loved.

                                 ❧ MARCIA JACOBER

*W*hile running a seminar on self-esteem, a therapist asked the group of adults if they thought their parents loved them as children. Most answered in the affirmative. Then she asked how many of them *felt loved* as children. Only a few hands were raised. Her point was obvious.

Parents may tell their children they are loved, but it's how we act toward them that shapes their self-esteem. How we speak to our children, what we say to them, how we touch them, all determine whether our children feel loved and worthy of being loved. Do we respect their wishes? Accept their shortcomings? Give them loving and playful attention? Or are we impatient when they speak? Do we act sometimes as if they are too difficult to bear?

When we treat our children with dignity and treat them like they matter, we are giving them one of the best gifts possible: self-esteem.

To feel whole, I must feel worthy of love. The same is true for my children.

142

All children wear the sign: "I want to be important NOW." Many of our juvenile delinquency problems arise because nobody reads the sign.

🖎 DAN PURSUIT

*O*ur attention is more vital to our children than food. They thrive on it. It makes them feel that they are important to us.

One way to give our children the attention they need is to actively listen to what they say. Active listening shows our children that we care. It shows them that we think what they have to say is important. However, our children's needs often outlasts our ability to listen. How can we let our children know that they are important NOW?

Sometimes a simple "good job," or "that's great" will suffice. Mostly, our children just need to know we are available to them.

When my actions show that I am available to my children, they are less demanding of my attention.

I am a part of all I have read.

🌀 JOHN KIERAN

*W*hy do mothers read so much? Why do we underline entire chapters of information? Why do we check out stacks of books from the library we know we'll never have time to read? The obvious reason is that we want to be well-informed, aware mothers.

But there is another reason. We look to the printed page to reflect our personal experience. We need new ways to articulate aspects of ourselves which are just beginning to form. In books and magazines, we try on images of mothers and motherhood like we might clothes in a dressing room. What fits? Which ones look good? Which ones are comfortable and leave room to grow? Which ones just aren't me? What we read helps us to conceptualize and comprehend the radical transformations we go through as we become full-fledged mothers.

Reading contributes to my self-knowledge. It helps me to understand myself better as I move through rapid change.

Crying

In the deserts of the heart
Let the healing fountain start.

                   ❧ W. H. AUDEN

Nothing makes a mother more nervous than a wailing infant. When the tears start and the tiny fists clench, our hearts leap into our throats. The screaming cries shake us to our core. We feel desperate. We realize that being strong doesn't mean we are unaffected by our infant's tears. They elicit a powerful maternal instinct: it hurts us to hear them cry.

Perhaps it would help to cry our own tears. Instead of keeping a stiff upper lip and becoming exasperated, we could allow ourselves to feel as helpless as our infant does; there is strength in that.

Sometimes crying is the strongest thing I can do.

*The natural rhythm of life is routine punctuated by
orgies.*

🖐 ALDOUS HUXLEY

*M*r. Huxley must be referring to life before
children. Now that we have children, "the
natural rhythm of life is routine punctuated by sleep."

Isn't it amazing that we used to be able to keep
night owl hours? Now we're in bed by nine o'clock
every night. Any deviation from the routine means
loss of precious sleep time.

And orgies? Sex isn't even in the routine, much less
orgies. The only action we see is coming from our
infant's orifices. Getting wild and crazy seems exciting only in the abstract. Even then, just thinking
about orgies exhausts us.

**How do I spell "energy crisis"?
M-O-T-H-E-R-H-O-O-D.**

*To talk to a child, to fascinate him, is much more
difficult than to win an electoral victory. But it is more
rewarding.*

👉 COLETTE

To fascinate a child, we must enter his world. We must listen intently to his words as they tell us who he is and how he perceives the world. If we respond in a way that tells him we see who he is, we will capture his attention. On the other hand, if we project our own perceptions onto his words, we will sever the connection. And we will have missed the chance to inhabit his world temporarily. Unless we want to "talk at him," we must put aside inhibitions and preconceptions and allow ourselves to be shaped by his inner life.

**I want to learn how to communicate in a way that
touches my child, and opens his universe to me.**

My husband dislikes housework and the mundane chores of child care and just refuses to participate. But since this is my job now, I feel guilty if I complain of his lack of support.

            ❧ ANONYMOUS MOTHER

*W*hy does this woman assume that all the child care and household responsibilities fall to her?

Assumptions can kill us. They can compromise our health, happiness, and sanity because they blind us from seeing our options. They preclude us from making necessary changes.

While we cannot always change another person, we *can* change ourselves. To begin with, we can question our assumptions about how we're supposed to be. We can make choices about our life instead of perpetuating beliefs and attitudes that do not serve us. By dismantling our assumptions, we create movement and movement creates room for change.

If I assume that there is nothing I can do to change myself or my situation, then chances are, nothing will change.

What one has to do usually can be done.

          ✑ ELEANOR ROOSEVELT

eing a single mother can seem like an insurmountable task. Often, we must be both "mother" and "father" to our children. We work to support our family while we single-handedly run a household. We pray a lot, asking for more strength, more time and more patience.

We enlist the help of our children. We assign them adult responsibilities as soon as they are able to handle them. Although we try not to, we often lean on them for emotional support. And we do our best to keep it all together.

I trust that "what I have to do can be done," especially if my child depends on it.

Happiness

When one door of happiness closes, another opens; but often we look so long at the closed door that we do not see the one which has been opened for us.

                           🌿 HELEN KELLER

*I*t isn't always easy to let go when one chapter of our life closes, and another chapter begins. We want things to continue to be the same forever, or at least wait until we are ready for change, but that is not how life works.

When one door closes, many others open. We are constantly confronted with new options. Sometimes, we feel like Alice, searching for the door that will lead us to Wonderland. And we will go through wrong doors and take many detours. But there are many doors to happiness, as long as I keep open to them.

If I stare at only one door, I will miss what all the others have to offer me.

Perhaps the most critical sexual abuse prevention strategy for parents is good communication with your children.

❧ NATIONAL CENTER ON CHILD ABUSE
AND NEGLECT

*T*hose of us who depend on others to care for our children often have difficulty finding someone with whom we feel comfortable. We worry about others mistreating or abusing our child.

Although we cannot always be with our child, we can be aware of his distress signals. We can pay attention to changes in his moods and behavior. When he randomly talks about the day, we can trust our intuition to tell us when something is not quite right.

We can ask simple questions such as, "Do you like your new babysitter?" "Does she ever do things you don't like?" "What do you do all day?" Although children have active imaginations, they rarely lie about sexual or physical abuse. We must trust what they tell us, not only with their words, but also with their eyes, gestures, and behavior. Otherwise, we can inadvertently betray them by our lack of vigilance.

By being totally in tune with my child, I can sense when something is wrong.

Children begin by loving their parents; as they grow older they judge them; sometimes they forgive them.
                  OSCAR WILDE

*P*art of growing up is discovering that our parents aren't perfect. The older we get, the more obvious are their faults—that is, until we become parents ourselves. Some of us immediately forgive our parents because we don't want to threaten our relationship. Others judge our parents harshly for their mistakes. Either way, our move toward independence and maturity is stymied.

If we gloss over our parents' shortcomings, we learn very little from their mistakes. If we hold on to judgment, our anger destroys us, not them.

To return to our parents as mature adults and parents in our own right, we must come to terms with who they are. If we can see them as separate individuals, then we will not need our anger to create separation, and we will not need illusions to keep our relationship intact.

To love my parents, I need not like everything about them. Genuine forgiveness can only come from genuine understanding.

When they are a few months old, they lie and look around and wave and smile and undergo a constant gentle agitation, as though they were sea anemones, gently waving in some other element, delicately responding to currents we cannot feel.

MARGARET DRABBLE

*O*nce outside the womb, a baby's delicate movements are reminiscent of our watery beginnings. For a time, they seem to float in a different element as they make the transition from the womb to the world. Watching them respond to unseen currents, we remember a gentle rocking and our mother's heartbeat; the soothing pulse of life. Although we have adapted to the world, often with a protective shell, a baby's presence can awaken a distant calm that still exists within us. If only for a moment, we remove our armor and experience the tender flesh inside.

To be vulnerable in a safe environment is to be open to life, open to love, and open to God.

We didn't inherit the land from our fathers. We are borrowing it from our children.

🖎 AMISH BELIEF

*T*oday more than ever, this belief needs to be heeded. We face monumental environmental problems, many of our own making: deforestation, global warming, famine, pollution, war, and poverty. It's a dismal picture that can overwhelm us, and make us doubt the future. We may even wonder whether we should have brought a child into this mess.

Yet, as mothers, we hope. Something inside assures us that, with ingenuity and love, change *is* possible. We owe it to the earth, and we owe it to our children.

I am responsible for finding new ways to help heal and protect this planet. By doing this, I am creating a better future for my children.

But ask now the beasts, and they shall teach thee;
and the fowls of the air, and they shall tell thee.

JOB 12:7

nfants have a natural affinity with animals.
Their arms and legs dance with excitement
whenever a dog or cat crosses their path. Even
the strangeness of the two-toed sloth or the arma-
dillo doesn't thwart the enthusiasm of babies.
Perhaps it's because infants, like animals, excel in
non-verbal communication.

It is up to us, as mothers, to nurture the innate love
and respect infants have for other living beings.

Children occasionally need the sort of benevolent neglect that allows a flower to choose its own time and place to blossom.

🌺 SALLY JAMES

*H*ow often have we felt like a court jester, constantly entertaining our children whether they welcomed it or not? "Trying too hard" is a trap all mothers fall into at one time or another. We know we've fallen into the trap whenever we find ourselves worrying that our children aren't "happy," or that we're "lousy parents." Have we forgotten that children need their own thoughts, and the freedom to choose their own games as much as they need to be entertained? Perhaps we need to stop trying to direct their moods and exercise "benevolent neglect." And give our children room to blossom in their own time.

I need to trust my inner barometer. It will tell me when my child needs active play with me, and when she needs to have her own adventures.

*The true secret of giving advice is, after you have
honestly given it, to be perfectly indifferent whether it
is taken or not and never persist in trying to set
people right.*

        ❧ HANNAH WHITALL SMITH

*M*any of us fail to be objective when we give
advice. We forget that the purpose of
advice is to provide options, not to dictate choices.
We become resentful if a person wants to think about
whether our advice is appropriate—instead of just
following it. Disguising control as advice is *not* the
best way to help a friend, because we then also take
responsibility for her actions—and for decisions
which are not ours to make.

Giving genuine advice is sharing our own experience; gently planting seeds which may or may not
blossom. We trust that the other person will make her
own decision. Although it's often tempting to provide
answers for others, we have to ask ourselves if we
really want to take responsibility for another's life
and, possibly, her mistakes.

**I can tell other mothers what worked for me. I
cannot tell them what will work for them.**

The course of true anything never does run smooth.
🖙 SAMUEL BUTLER

*T*he things that mean the most to us rarely go as
planned. We run into inconvenient detours
which, at first, seem like obstacles. However, they are
often adventures for learning that enrich our lives.

If we are rigid in our need for control, we don't see
a turn of events as an opportunity to explore new
avenues. Life revolts, and we take it personally. Where
has our spontaneity gone? Have our plans crowded
out the possibility of serendipity? The unplanned,
unexpected events add color to the tapestry of life.

**All the energy I put into warding off life's
alterations could be used to enjoy the surprises
that await me each day.**

Don't kid yourself. Those women [on Jane Fonda's exercise tape] have never had babies. Their children were all born by professional stunt women.

              DAVE BARRY

*P*regnancy and childbirth give our bodies a work out. Most of us gain weight, get a few stretch marks, and have our breast size altered. We stare at our bodies in the mirror wondering if we'll ever look the way we did before. How will we ever manage to get ourselves back into shape?

Then there are those of us who look like we never had babies. Just months after giving birth, we can wear tight shorts and swimming suits. We don't need a postpartum wardrobe. People wonder if we did the birthing, or hired a stunt woman.

Whatever category we fit into, we must remember one thing: all of us performed the same miracle.

My body did what it needed to do. To help it heal and recover, I must respect it for what it has so wonderfully achieved.

Those who do not remember the past are condemned to repeat it.

❧ GEORGE SANTAYANA

Some of our mothers felt bound and gagged by motherhood. They felt victimized, often because they felt they didn't have a choice. In their misery, they often blamed us. They refused to take responsibility for their own feelings and choices. It was always something or someone out there that created their problems.

Those of us with a mother like this know the impact she had on our lives. Leaving home and having our own child do not automatically give us the psychological understanding to be an emotionally healthier and more mature parent. We must unlearn our mother's patterns and learn more constructive ways to deal with our feelings and the consequences of our actions. Otherwise, like our mother, we will turn our children into lightning rods for our pain.

I am not condemned by my past, but I need to consciously work not to duplicate it.

Out of the strain of the Doing,
Into the peace of the Done.

           JULIA LOUISE WOODRUFF

One constant fact of motherhood: we go all day long. Our day can start any time, especially if we have an infant, and once it starts we're off and running.

As a massage therapist once told me, as I slumped down on her table, "We mothers use our adrenal glands all day, even though our bodies are meant to use them only for an hour each day. That's like having your foot on the gas *all day long*!"

No wonder that after the children have gone to sleep, we sigh as we shift gears. We move "out of the strain of the doing, and into the peace of the done."

I need the peace and contentment each day's ending offers me.

Advice is what we ask for when we already know the answer but wish we didn't.

ERICA JONG

Sometimes we ask for advice when what we really want is to ask for help. Afraid others might think we're weak, we disguise our wishes and ask indirect questions. If we're lucky, the other person figures out what we want and offers her assistance.

Sometimes we blame others for being insensitive when they don't read our minds and anticipate our needs. Perhaps instead of manipulating people to do what we want, we could try asking directly.

Asking for help does not mean that I am going to get what I want, but at least my honesty gives others a clue to what I need.

Everyone must row with the oars he has.

        ❧ ENGLISH PROVERB

*A*s mothers, we compare ourselves to other mothers. We try to model ourselves after the mothers we respect. When our lives don't look like theirs, however, we feel like failures. We forget that we aren't the same people, living in the same house, with the same bank account.

Our children, too, are different, and they challenge us in different ways. The circumstances of their births, the level of their needs, and the diversity of their personalities, all create unique scenarios that must be dealt with in a way that is fitting for them. We must "row with the oars we have." They'll probably prevent the boat from going adrift.

There are two sides to every oar.

You feel so much love for your first child that you wonder how you could possibly love the second one as much. Then you discover how infinite your capacity to love is.

                  🖐 LINDA D'AGROSA

With the birth of our first child, we are initiated into motherhood. And with this passage, we are introduced to a depth of love beyond all measure. Like a beam of concentrated light, we focus this love on our little one; we surround him with it.

For many of us, such abundant love is unfamiliar. Because it is new, we wonder if it has any limits. Could we possibly love our next child as much? It's hard to imagine we could feel as deeply for someone else, especially someone we haven't met yet. What if there are limits to our caring? We fear that love might be finite and we will be spread too thin. In spite of our doubts, we have our second child and discover that love has no boundaries.

Our first child helps us to discover the depth of love; our second child, the breadth of it.

I know that you believe you understand what you think I said, but I am not sure you realize that what you heard is not what I meant.

🐝 BERRY AND HOMER INC.

Nothing is more frustrating than a breakdown in communication. We don't feel heard; we know our words aren't getting through; and we can't find the right words to express our thoughts and feelings. Our partner says he hears us, yet his response indicates that he doesn't get it. Instead of bringing us closer, our words alienate. We hit a brick wall.

To find out what went wrong, we might ask ourselves: "At what point in the conversation did communication breakdown?" "Did my words strike a defensive chord?" "Did I expect him to 'read my mind'?" "Did I listen and try to find a better way to express myself?" Perhaps I should let the subject rest and try again another time.

Sometimes I need to remember that communication involves two parts: speaking *and* listening.

Surprises

Don't be discouraged if you are unable to diagnose your child's illnesses. The number and variety of childhood illnesses are staggering; that's why there are pediatricians.

✍ CHRISTINE CIAVARELLA

Mothers never quite know what to expect. Our infant's stools change color, his nose runs and then it stops running. He cries for no apparent reason. Infant acne, diaper rash, viral rash, roseola, hives . . . . it's all so confusing. We try to guess. Should he be seen by a doctor? Is this normal for a baby his age? Is this a life-threatening disease or a simple cold? Are these mysterious symptoms related to teething? Just when we think we've figured everything out, the picture changes.

With the advent of motherhood, we have to become amateur doctors, lawyers, psychologists, nutritionists and fashion consultants. The last is the biggest surprise of all—especially when we can't even get ourselves dressed before eleven o'clock.

As a mother, I can't expect myself to know everything. However, I must expect myself to know when to call the pediatrician.

A camel is a horse designed by a committee.
          🐪 ANONYMOUS

*E*ver notice how many ad hoc committees approach mothers? Each one tries to tell us how to best design our baby. There's "The Relative Committee," "The Friendly Neighbor Committee," "The Here's-What-I-Did-To-My-Child Committee," "The Expert-On-Everything Committee," and numerous others. They don't care if we're members, they just want us to implement their findings and follow their guidelines. Luckily, mothers know how to graciously nod, then do what we were going to do in the first place. If we tried to incorporate everything every committee prescribes, we'd get a camel instead of a child!

Tact is the best way to steer a committee.

My second child was so different from my first,
I practically had to learn everything all over again.
                               TERRI DAWSON

What an adventure we undertake every time we have another baby! With the birth of each child come different challenges and adjustments. Our first born may have refused to sit in the car seat; our second may prefer to sit alone in the bouncer chair mesmerized by colorful toys. The methods for putting one baby to sleep only make another squirm and fuss.

It is important to respect each child's individuality and be sensitive to each one's needs. Being a committed parent means having the courage to explore uncharted territory. We must be pioneers, often without a compass. Being open to learning everything all over again is not easy, but the rewards are great. The course we choose is up to us.

I can look upon each child as a welcome challenge or I can habitually tread the beaten path. Which will it be?

*Marriage is the deep, deep peace of the double bed
after the hurly-burly of the chaise lounge.*

      ❧ MRS. PATRICK CAMPBELL

*T*he introduction of a baby into a marriage forever changes that marriage. As Anne Morrow
Lindbergh writes in *Gift from the Sea*, "One resents
any change, even though one knows that transforma-
tion is natural and part of the process of life and its
evolution. Like its parallel in physical passion, the
early ecstatic stage of a relationship cannot continue
always at the same pitch of intensity."

Initially, many of us cannot accept the "deep, deep
peace of the double bed" and we mistake it for death.
We are not yet comfortable with our new identity as
mothers—and as parents. But try and try as we might,
we cannot resurrect our former self. We have moved
into a new phase of our lives and we can never go
back. Together with our spouses, we have assumed
responsibility for another life, and that *is* going to
change the nature of our relationship. Now we must
be both lovers *and* parents.

**Instead of trying to resurrect my old self, I can
integrate it with who I am now. The "hurly-burly"
is still part of me, but I now have the opportunity
to be much more.**

Never cut what you can untie.

🖎 JOSEPH JOUBERT

*W*e all grew up with the old saying, "Patience is a virtue." The value of patience was instilled in us even though we realized that it was lacking in quite a few of its proponents. Many of those around us were cutting things they should have untied.

While some of us were born patient, others of us have to cultivate this worthwhile talent. Our children can be our finest teachers. With them, we learn to be patient even when we don't really want to be. For our children's sake, we must repeatedly untie things we would just as soon cut. This enables us to appreciate things we might otherwise rush through. It also helps us to realize that a quick temper can stifle our infant's budding curiosity and make him feel inadequate as he explores each knot.

Patience requires that I give myself and others the time to figure out how to best untie each knot.

Blues are the songs of despair, but gospel songs are the songs of hope.

MAHALIA JACKSON

Gospel songs are "prayer in action." They have a rich tradition that is tried and true. As we raise our voices, our spirits are raised, and our hope is restored.

Mothers do a lot of praying. Sometimes, it's all we can do. Perhaps we remember a special hymn from church, or we create our own music of hope. Occasionally, we'll "sing the blues," but we can always come back to the spirituals that drench our souls with sunshine.

Prayer isn't only words, it's also music.

Listening

Listening is a magnetic and strange thing, a creative force. The friends who listen to us are the ones we move toward, and we want to sit in their radius. When we are listened to, it creates us, makes us unfold and expand.

                          ❧ KARL MENNINGER

When we think of our closest friends, we usually think of those who listen to us. We think of those people in whom we can confide our deepest secrets and wildest dreams without fear of judgment.

Friends who listen are not preoccupied with changing us. Our being responds to their listening presence and we allow our essence to emerge. When we are listened to, it "creates us and makes us unfold and expand." By being listened to, we can hear ourselves and come to know ourselves better.

Listening is a creative force. I owe it to myself to find time to listen and to be listened to.

I don't know the key to success, but the key to failure is trying to please everybody.

🐾 BILL COSBY

*P*eople pleasing is an indulgence mothers can ill afford. Not only do we compromise our own integrity, but we unwittingly sacrifice our children if we try to make them into what other people think they should be. For instance, Grandpa is incensed that we allow our child to leave the dinner table before the adults are through. "You'll spoil him," he warns. When we do not stand up for what we think is best for our children, we fail them.

People-pleasing is a trap we all fall into from time to time. We want to be liked and we don't want to rock the boat. We don't want to be confrontational, but we must know when to draw the line. We must know when the needs of our children surpass the needs others may have for them to behave in a particular way.

When I try to please everybody, I compromise my integrity, my children, and my values.

There was such speed in her little body,
And such lightness in her footfall.

              JOHN CROWE RANSOM

*I*nfants are robust. There is so much speed and movement in their little bodies. We can hardly keep up. But not to worry. A group of world class athletes mimicked every move one baby made. Every little jerk of her arms and legs, every excited wriggle, every attempt to roll over, and every gurgle and cry was emulated by these super athletes. After four hours, the athletes were exhausted. They had to stop. But the infant kept on going.

Motherhood is a marathon that puts us in a class by ourselves.

There is such a thing as too much couth.

           ❧ S. J. PERELMAN

*U*nlike adults, children could care less about couth. They fling carrots and peas against the walls, they eat disgusting things off the ground, they grab their crotches whenever they get the chance, and they probably have more fun than we do.

When was the last time we sprayed a friend with the sink hose? Had a food fight? Sucked jell-o through a straw? Every one of us needs to let loose. We need to extricate ourselves from restrictive social graces, especially when we're in danger of developing "too much couth." If we're rusty, all we need to do is interact with our little bohemians for a while. Then, if we're not too far gone, it'll all come back to us.

Too much couth is one of the hazards of life; a bit of folly is one of the joys.

A family that plays together, stays together.

*🖎*ANONYMOUS

*P*eople are working more hours per day than ever before, and when they're not working they're often recovering from work. Whether our vocation is fulfilling or not, the fact is, we spend most of our waking hours at work.

Not surprisingly, we are often too burned out to play. When we want rest, even play feels like work. We forget how rejuvenating it can be.

Play refreshes our minds and bodies. If our relationship with our spouse is strained, play helps us to soften and let go of unnecessary grudges. Children love it when we let down and play with them. Play brings us close and it lets our kids know that no matter how busy we get, we always have time for them.

I must not forget to play. I need it and my children do, too.

Choices

The difficulty in life is the choice.

🐛 GEORGE MOORE

*M*ost of us want to have it all. The trouble is we want it all now. Our abundance of options either paralyzes us or we scramble to attain everything at once. Either way, we preclude ourselves from choosing what is clearest and best for us.

It is helpful to remember that our most important life choices emerge slowly. Sometimes we are struck suddenly with an insight, but more often than not, choices simmer inside until they are ready to be born.

Once one choice calls out more clearly than others, I will be able to actualize it.

No human being can really understand another, and
no one can arrange another's happiness.

            ✌ GRAHAM GREENE

 here is it written that mothers know precisely
who their children are? Just as we go through
profound inner changes, so do our children. They go
through phases and inner processes that do not
involve us. Whether we like it or not, their journey is
separate from ours. They must seek to know themselves, just as we have sought self-knowledge. They
must arrange their own happiness.

At times, we will feel estranged from our children.
We may not always know how to interpret what is
happening behind their eyes. One day, we may look
back and more fully understand the subtle changes
we sensed were happening. Yet some mystery always
remains.

**I will never understand my child one hundred and
fifty percent.**

I lost touch with my "other selves"—wife, friend, co-worker. I did not feel good about myself and even sometimes resented the kids for preventing me from being in an adult world.

☜ ANONYMOUS MOTHER

*M*any of us thrive on challenges that are available only in the adult world. Our careers are extremely important to us.

The repetitive demands of motherhood frequently leave us feeling one-dimensional. Although we love our children and we love being mothers, we also need more. Were we to confine ourselves to "one self," we would feel resentful. Eventually, we might view our children as impediments to our growth and success.

Each of us needs to be honest with ourselves. We need to make decisions based on who we are, and what our real needs are. We need not limit ourselves to one definition of mother when many options exist.

Being a mother and being a career woman are not mutually exclusive pursuits.

What nature delivers to us is never stale. Because what nature creates has eternity in it.

ISAAC BASHEVIS SINGER

Adoption is a celebrated event. For whatever reason our child has been delivered to us, it is a miracle. Although we did not physically experience the gestation of an embryo, we were filled with anticipation. Our innate desire and love for this little being that has come to us, instead of through us, helped to bring our child into a safe and loving world. We are stewards to a new life and we celebrate nature's sacred creation. This child was meant to be held in our arms.

My child is a most wanted child. Eternity is in his eyes.

Madness need not be all breakdown. It may also be breakthrough.

❧ R. D. LAING

*J*ust like infants and children, mothers experience times of traumatic change and overwhelming internal adjustments. We feel crazy, and our madness seems to be without purpose. Fortunately, "madness need not be all breakdown."

Ever notice how an infant cries excessively and becomes irritable right before a developmental breakthrough? Ever notice how a child seems restless until he passes through a certain stage of growth? Adults experience the same thing.

For a while, we feel a lack of centeredness, and we may experience excessive anxiety until the actual moment of breakthrough. We float in an uncomfortable limbo until the deeper currents of our lives settle.

Knowing this is all part of the process of change and growth may not help me to feel less crazy, but it can help me understand that I'm not.

Be like the bird
That passing in her
flight
A while on boughs too silent,
Feels them give way
Beneath her and yet sings,
Knowing she hath wings.

🖐 VICTOR HUGO

*C*hange often feels like "boughs too slight." Yet, when we accept that nothing in life is a guarantee, a truce can be called and inner peace established. It's not like we're thrown to the whims of fate. We all have free will which can be exercised at any time. When our will is in harmony with the changing currents around us, our lives are more content. We realize we have choices and can see the results of our actions in terms of a larger picture.

**Children bring change. If I go with the change,
I will be a better dance partner with life.**

My partner often says, "Let's make up and go to bed."
That's the damnedest thing. Why would I want to
make love with someone I don't like at the moment?

ANONYMOUS

"Making up" before we have dealt with our feelings often leads to more of those same feelings. Of course, we can gloss over or deny bad feelings with a quick "making up," but the feelings won't go away. Most likely, they will resurface somewhere down the line.

If we don't respect our own feelings how can we expect our spouse to? Sure, he is being disrespectful, but so are we. In our haste to resolve complex issues, we jump ahead to "the good part." But until we deal with our true feelings, the "good part" won't feel so good.

Quick fixes leave me feeling empty and compromised. There is another option: I can respect my true feelings and deal with them appropriately.

The psychic scars caused by believing that you are ugly leave a permanent mark on your personality.
                                JOAN RIVERS

We live in a culture that places a disproportionate amount of value on physical beauty. Not only do we tend to discount inner beauty, but we have a limited view of what constitutes real beauty. As a result, many of us grow up thinking we're ugly, or simply, "not pretty enough." Many of our parents were influenced by the cultural standards and their words reinforced the norm and left psychic scars.

I hope I may be different with my children. I see the inner beauty and radiance they possess. And I tell them. If we are in touch with our beauty, it will show.

I see beauty in my child. I am beginning to see it in myself.

False Sense of Security

*I'm a professional balker. I'm very afraid of change.
I'm the type of person that if I fall into a rut, I'll start
hanging pictures, move in, and make it a home.*
> 🖎 SAM MEIER (SERENITY SAM)

*H*ow many of us mistake falling into a rut for security? Do we view change as an annoying inconvenience or a horrible experience to be avoided at all cost?

It is all too easy for mothers to fall into a rut. Our responsibilities at work and at home can overwhelm us. They can negatively determine the course of our lives unless we initiate change. But change seems to take too much effort. We are afraid to relinquish our illusion of security, so we take refuge in convenience and the "known." We probably need to ask ourselves what is so great about the rut we live in now.

**If I think change is hard, I should try living with
my false security for a while.**

A few years ago, had someone called me an Indispensable Woman, I would have considered it a compliment. Today, I know better.

                    🌰 ELLEN SUE STERN

*M*others know how to get things done. We're masters at organizing lists and juggling schedules. We have a remarkable ability to take an abstract problem and break it down into concrete steps. We get results. Because we are so efficient, we sometimes forget to delegate responsibility and we end up doing everything ourselves. We become "Indispensable Women." No one can do anything for us because we're the only ones who can do it right.

When we force others into a dependent role, they resent us for it. And our overdeveloped sense of responsibility makes others weary. Luckily we can't continue at this pace forever. We eventually burn out and learn to share the burden.

Is my self-worth dependent on my indispensability? It needn't be.

*I refused to believe that motherhood was second-rate
or not a spiritual path in itself. My children were
not holes in me but openings, unwitting teachers on
this nameless path.*

      ❧ CHINA GALLAND

*I*n women's efforts to emancipate ourselves and
prove we were equal to men, we became too
eager to trade the rich experience of motherhood for
the benefits of a career. Motherhood was considered
second-rate. Instead of a woman's success being
narrowly defined as "getting married and having
children," our success became narrowly defined as
"becoming a C.E.O. before we were forty."

We soon discovered that both stereotypes were too
confining. They excluded our individual identity and
left little room for us to realize our unique dreams.
Anne Morrow Lindbergh poses an essential question:
"Why have we been seduced into abandoning this
timeless inner strength of woman for the temporal
outer strength of man?" Why indeed?

**When I abandon my inner strength, I abandon the
path with a heart, and instead tread an unfulfilling
course.**

Miracles do not happen? It's a miracle if they don't.
ANDREW LANG

No one expects an apparently healthy child to become seriously ill. But it happens! Days, weeks or months after our baby is born, we find ourselves rushing to the hospital with an ailing child. We are so thrown off by the urgency of the event that we are paralyzed. How could this have happened so suddenly, without any warning?

We fear we will lose our child as quickly as she came into our lives. We hope. We pray. We ask for a miracle. A miracle is delivered. Our child lives.

When we're spared the loss of our child, we're immediately freed from the terror that engulfed us—and that is a miracle.

Character contributes to beauty. It fortifies a woman as her youth fades. A mode of conduct, a standard of courage, discipline, fortitude and integrity can do a great deal to make a woman beautiful.

                ❧ JACQUELINE BISSET

Motherhood is empowering. It helps us to become more resolved and better focused. Limited time and additional demands encourage us to be selective about the direction of our life. We're able to better distinguish between real options and false ones.

Although the beauty of our youth may fade, the beauty of womanhood emerges with a new maturity. The wisdom of experience shines in our eyes. No longer simply skin deep, our beauty reflects a deepening of our inner lives. It reflects our intelligence, discipline, and courage. Our beauty encompasses the richness and depth of our experience of womanhood.

The beauty of experience is the beauty that lasts; it is the beauty of my whole self.

Sympathy

That kid is trying to kill me!

❧ ANONYMOUS MOTHER

*Y*ou'd think children had better things to do than plan their mothers' demise. Just as we think they've settled into a workable schedule—one that might meet everyone's needs—they change it.

Our friends tell us to relax, go with the flow. Of course, that's easier said than done. How can we tell them there is no flow? How can we expect them to understand the restless nights, the constant interruptions? How can we convince them that our children are far better at waking up during the night than we are at putting them back to sleep?

Will our friends ever realize that a mother's life is ruled by a drooling midget?! Probably not until they have kids. . . .

When I'm looking for sympathy, I'd better look for the right people in the right places.

Why do I always apologize about everything, all the time?

🖎 LORRIE MINTZ

*M*others usually have an overdeveloped sense of responsibility. Because we're responsible for *everything*, we become defensive. Somehow we feel responsible for all the chaos and turmoil baby's new presence creates, and we're constantly apologizing. If our baby cries, we apologize. If dinner is late, we apologize.

We must remember that we are not all-powerful. The baby isn't crying or sick *because* of us. We're not the source of the problem and we are not always in control.

Just because we gave birth to them doesn't mean that everything they do is our fault!

You have to take the time to be a whole person if you want to rear your children to be whole.
　　　　　　　　　DELLA WHITE STEELE

ontrary to what many of us were raised to believe, devoting every minute of every day to our children does not make us complete mothers. To raise whole children, we must be whole. If we sacrifice ourselves for our children, giving up our own identity, they will learn how to be dependent, not self-sufficient.

To be whole, we need to take time for ourselves, time to nurture our bodies, and time to nurture our minds. We need to replenish what we put out. We need others to cuddle and hold us. We need solitude, time with our friends, and time to regroup so we may come at the challenges of motherhood from a place of strength—from a place of wholeness.

I will be an example for my child. Meeting my own needs will help my children to learn how to meet their own needs.

Cleaning your house while your kids are still growing is like shoveling the walk before it stops snowing.
      ❧ MARY KAY BLAKELY

*E*ver wonder why we bother to clean up after our little ones when we know the place will be a mess in minutes? One reason we are constantly straightening is because we need a sense of accomplishment. Since long-term projects are out of the question, it helps to turn our attention to more manageable goals: washing a dish or two, wiping down the counters, scrubbing the toilet bowl.

A crowded house means a crowded mind. If we put our house in order it helps to curb the "psychic clutter" in our lives. The cans stacked in the cupboards, the toilet paper on the roll bring a little stability and order. Cleaning the house reassures us that we have not joined the ranks of the organizationally impaired.

Cleaning has a therapeutic value. It just might prevent me from ending up on the psychiatrist's couch.

Roses are red, violets are blue,
I'm a schizophrenic, and so am I.

🖎 FRANK CROW

*I*nfants' mood swings can make us feel schizophrenic. One minute our child is crying, the next minute he's bubbling with laughter. One minute he's angry, nothing satisfies him. The next minute he's enamored with a shiny toy. He seems no worse for the wear; we're wrecks.

Because we are so close to our child, we take the emotional roller coaster rides with him. Painful bouts with teething, illness, and clingy phases can leave us mentally off-balance and emotionally drained. However, as he approaches toddlerhood, we learn to be a little more detached. Instead of responding immediately, we learn to hover until he settles on a mood of choice. This way, we do not perpetuate transient moods, and he still feels responded to and loved.

Learning to be detached at the appropriate times is a sane and healthy thing for mothers to do.

Obligations

There are two reasons for doing things—a very good reason and the real reason.

ANONYMOUS

How many of us feel guilty when we say no? How many of us do things we'd rather not do, simply because we feel obligated? How often are we torn between "a very good reason" and "the real reason"?

We all do things out of a sense of duty. We all have unpleasant obligations. However, if we constantly place ourselves second and fail to stand up for ourselves, we compromise our own integrity. And we begin to resent others' demands.

When we stop trying to please everyone, we'll have fewer obligations—and more respect.

Since I've started saying no to the things I'm supposed to do, the more time I have to do the things I want to do.

Every calling is great when greatly pursued.
               OLIVER WENDALL HOLMES, JR.

*E*veryone of us has great ideas—a house we want to design, a concert we want to perform, a business we want to start, children we want to raise. But we get bogged down in details. We allow ourselves to be distracted by small things, perhaps because deep down, we don't really believe we can attain our ideals. We lack self-confidence.

In our uncertainty, we make excuses. We pretend that it doesn't matter. But it does matter. Whatever we choose to do, we must "pursue greatly." Otherwise, our goals will lose their meaning, and we will lose a vital part of our being—our inspiration.

What I choose is not as important as that I choose it—and that I pursue it fully.

If one is not going to take the necessary precautions to avoid having parents, one must undertake to bring them up.

🕭 QUENTIN CRISP

O ur parents may not admit it, but most of us raised them as much as we were raised by them. Now that we have our own children, our task is over, right? Wrong. As sure as the sun rises, our parents will be watching how we raise our children, and comparing it with their style. They will be critical of differences and will announce self-righteously, "I did such and such when you were a baby, and you turned out just fine!"

Before we tell them about the mental anguish we suffered, the hours of therapy we endured, and the fingernails we chewed off, we must remember one thing: since we didn't take the necessary precautions to avoid having them, we must undertake to bring our parents up, once again.

Raising children, raising parents, raising consciousness—it's all the same thing, and it never ends.

The only reason I would take up jogging is so that I could hear heavy breathing again.

ERMA BOMBECK

t is far too easy for us mothers to neglect the needs of our bodies. We're too tired to brush our teeth, much less swim in the nude. At some point after we've delivered a baby, we need to take steps to feel comfortable in our body again. We need to find ways to feel connected to each of our senses: touch, smell, hearing, sight. We need to feel the flow of our desire and the heat of our passion.

It is essential that we keep our sensuality alive. It is the root of our creative force, and the heart of our spirituality.

My sensuality may be submerged but it is still available to me. I need to reclaim it.

At any given moment, life is completely senseless. But viewed over a period, it seems to reveal itself as an organism existing in time, having a purpose, tending in a certain direction.

ℚ ALDOUS HUXLEY

*H*aving a baby is such an abrupt change, it can make us feel suspended in time. Our routines are disrupted; all our plans are put on hold. By the look of it, life appears to be completely senseless.

Reflecting on the past, especially when we feel adrift, can give us perspective. As we stand with one foot in the present, and one foot in the past, images arise—our childhood wallpaper or the three-foot-tall view of a teacher's feet. As the frames of our life come together in a mosaic, we sense a purpose and a direction. We see how we got from there to here.

To make sense of my life, I must often step back and look at the whole.

The man who has no inner life is the slave of his circumstances.

🖎 HENRI FREDERIC AMIEL

*P*rolonged stress can lock us into a cycle of depression. It can cut us off from our center at a time when we need it most. We become despondent, unable to cope, and we feel like victims.

It is essential for us to replenish the energy we put into mothering. Each of us must find ways that are conducive to a contemplative drawing together of the self, and engage in activities that contribute to our inner life.

Turning inward is not an escape. When we go inside ourselves, we discover we are limitless and our spirit extends out into the universe. What better way to combat stress and liberate ourselves from the shackles of our circumstances?

Stress severs me from life. Nourishing my spirit connects me to life.

Fond as we are of our loved ones, there comes at times during their absence an unexplained peace.

ANNE SHAW

We've all become accustomed to noise—traffic, television, children. Fond as we are of the noise of our little ones, it is wonderful when we are left alone in the house. It may take us a while to notice the unfamiliar silence in our ears. We can't believe that everyone is truly gone. Yet, when the quiet finally sinks in, our being expands into the luxury of peace.

The peace of solitude .... I have yet to find its equal.

She did observe with some dismay, that, far from conquering all, love lazily sidestepped practical problems.

❧ JEAN STAFFORD

*L*ove conquers all. At least, that's what we're told. While love has many magnificent abilities, it doesn't solve the daily problems, like getting along, for example. Just because we love someone doesn't mean we always like their habits. This becomes even more obvious when we have children.

Different parenting styles, different priorities, different expectations of who does what, all create tension that must be worked out. Fortunately, this is where love steps in. When we can keep in touch with the love we share, problem-solving becomes a team effort. We strive to be fair, considerate, flexible and supportive—and so does our spouse.

Love may not conquer all my practical problems, but it makes me more committed to resolving them.

*I came to the conclusion then that continual
mindfulness . . . must mean, not a sergeant-major-like
drilling of thoughts, but a continual readiness to look
and readiness to accept whatever came.*

🖎 JOANNA FIELD

*A*s parents, we will be confronted with many uncomfortable dilemmas. How do we insure our children's safety without restricting them unnecessarily?

Children can no longer ride their bikes across town without adult supervision. Halloween has become a nightmare. The number of child abductions is continually on the rise. How do we respond? How can we be cautious without being paranoid? How do we raise our children to be careful, not fearful?

"Continual mindfulness" is a kind of readiness; a mental preparedness that alerts us to danger without reacting prematurely. It helps us to use our best judgment *in the moment*.

When I transform my fear into "mindfulness," I can make more balanced decisions about my children's safety.

Growth

Then I began to realize that I had to take another step in my evolution and growth.

❧ EILEEN CADDY

*E*ver notice how children grow? How they move from one phase to the next, propelled by some inner rhythm? Evolution moves through them as naturally as a current in a river.

Evolution is a constant in all of our lives. Although we may try to stifle it or resist its course, it keeps on moving, undaunted. When we resist its urges, it patiently waits for us to catch up. When we are ready "to take the next step," it is there, at the threshold, to meet us. Initially, we may experience some turbulence. Yet after we advance into our growth, we wonder what took us so long. What were we afraid of?

When I willingly take steps in my own evolution, life is less like walking on hot coals and more like a dance.

Contributions to the common good are not measured in dollars, hours, or labor. They are measured in love.
❧ DELLA WHITE STEELE

*I*ntellectually, all of us share this view. However, our emotions tell another story. Those of us who are accustomed to financially supporting ourselves and our family, are uncomfortable with the dependency motherhood brings. We begin to feel like maternal freeloaders.

Those of us who choose to remain at home, feel guilty spending "our husband's" money on groceries, baby clothes, and stamps. But, we feel *especially* guilty whenever we spend "his" hard-earned money on ourselves.

In time, we may be able to find income-producing projects we can integrate with childrearing. However, what is more important is that we begin to measure our contributions, not in dollars and cents, but in love. Unless we ourselves recognize the value of our mothering, we will continue to devalue it, as society does, because it doesn't produce income.

Mothering is my contribution to the "common good." What better offering can I give the world?

[Children] do not grow gradually. They move forward in spurts like the hands of clocks in railway stations.
                    CYRIL CONNOLLY

*B*abies are not the same from day to day or week to week. Like all great works, they have an incubation period which may or may not be visible. Then, overnight, they change.

Some of us are frustrated by this erratic growth. Deep down, we believe that mothers should always know who their children are. We should always sense what is going on with them.

Maybe we need to shatter the myth of "The All-Knowing-Mother." No matter how keenly we observe their inner stirrings, we cannot always detect the subtle and complex changes that blossom into growth spurts. We need to accept that our little ones, too, have more than an ounce of mystery.

ESP is not a given for mothers. If I pay attention to the moods and behaviors of my child, I'll catch on, sooner or later.

A child is a curly, dimpled lunatic.

                          RALPH WALDO EMERSON

Children are silly lunatics, full of the howling moon. They vocalize their existence around the house. They announce their euphoric presence to the cat. They hold titillating conversations with beings we cannot see. Imagination rules on their planet and dreams are as real as the sidewalk beneath their unsteady legs. They are not limited by the rational mind or logical ideas. Their vision extends out into the universe.

Many of us wish we felt as our children do. As new mothers, we can't find the time and energy to tend to our inventive and artistic projects. Maybe we can look to the moon as a source of creative inspiration. As a photographer professor once told me: "The moon develops the imagination in the same way that photographs come to life in a chemical bath." Could it be that lunatics aren't crazy, just inspired?

My child has a direct line to the source of creation. Like her, I can find inspiration all around me.

Discipline is guidance, not punishment. You are teaching what is appropriate behavior and what is inappropriate.

          🖎 DOT HATTICH

*C*hildren need structure and limits. They look to us to set boundaries. How we do this will determine whether our children's self-esteem remains intact.

Although we may not always like their behavior, they must know they are always worthy of our love. If we punish and scold, and constantly make our children 'behave,' we give them the message that they are not acceptable the way they are. We attach our child's worth to his actions if we say "bad boy" when he doesn't obey our commands, and "good boy" when he does what we want. We need to offer our children at least one "yes" for every "no."

Discipline is not punishment. Discipline is guidance with love.

Guidance provides a living example of how to live.

Nothing on earth consumes more quickly than the passion of resentment.

👉 ECCE HOMO

s much as we'd like to believe otherwise, babies create stress in a marriage. They put it to the test.

We depend on our spouse in ways we have never had to before. We expect him to share the responsibilities of parenthood. And we expect household chores to be evenly distributed, especially if we work outside the home. In trying to establish what is fair, words like "always" and "never" enter our vocabulary with incredible frequency. "I *always* put our son to bed." "You *never* give him a bath." Our anger builds and, if we let it, hardens into resentment. Like a wall it isolates us from our spouse even though we live under the same roof. Unless we take steps to resolve inequities, our marriage may suffer.

Resentment separates, communication unites.

Today, the shrapnel from my anger scattered indiscriminately, hitting the people I love.

❧ BARBARA MOORE

*A*ll of us get angry with ourselves. We get angry when we feel we've handled a situation poorly or allowed someone to take advantage of us. There's always something we should have said differently or done better.

When we turn our anger in on ourselves, we are unable to forgive our shortcomings, we are unable to forgive ourselves for not doing it better. Our anger festers, whittling away at our self-worth. The pain we cause ourselves distorts our interactions with others, especially those who are closest to us. We project our anger onto others, seeing them as the source of our pain.

When we realize that the problem is not our anger but how we handle it, then we can begin to make changes. Instead of allowing our anger to destroy us and damage our relationships with those we love, we can express it before it reaches a deadly crescendo.

Turning my anger in and blasting it out is destructive to myself and others. It is a relief to know there are alternatives.

Democracy is a small core of common agreement,
surrounded by a rich variety of differences.

                JAMES BRYANT CONANT

*F*amilies are very much like governments. A democratic system respects the rights of the individual. It has faith in the human spirit. A democracy does not assume that only one individual knows what is right for the collective whole. It strives to bring out the best in everyone by allowing a rich variety of differences.

A dictatorship, on the other hand, does not have faith in the wisdom of its people. It rules by fear and control and does not allow individual differences. It restricts the creative expression and intelligence of everyone within its structure to ensure its own survival. Only a remarkable few flourish within this system.

It is up to me to decide which type of family structure I will create.

God gave burdens, also shoulders.

🖎 YIDDISH PROVERB

*B*urdens are a part of life. Fortunately, so are shoulders. Under extreme circumstances, we tap unimaginable resources and realize just how strong our shoulders are. Our strength becomes our pride.

Eventually, however, burdens weigh us down. Like a workhorse hitched to a plow, we become accustomed to the weight of the yoke. Because we can handle it, we take on more than our share and expect ourselves to perform like superwomen.

Being strong is certainly one of women's greatest attributes. Yet we must choose our burdens carefully.

**"Strength" does not mean I have to do it all myself.
There is also strength in asking for help, and in
knowing my own limits.**

*Each woman is being made to feel it is her own
cross to bear if she can't be the perfect clone of the
male superman and the perfect clone of the feminine
mystique.*

                              BETTY FRIEDAN

*I*n today's world, mothers are expected to excel
   at everything. Society expects it of us and we
expect it of ourselves. Yet being the high-powered
career woman who is also the perfect mother and
hostess looks much more attractive from a distance
than it does up-close. In fact, it feels more like glam-
orized slavery than a desirable way to live.

Many of us strive to be this illusionary person nevertheless. We think something is wrong with *us*
whenever we cannot be part superwoman and part
feminine mystique. Could it be that something is
wrong with the image, not us?

**Isn't it time I recognized that the expectations put
on women are a prescription for early death?**

It was so snug and warm there, and the feeding was automatic.... No wonder the memory of those accommodations lingered in the blood and nerves of everyone. It was dark, yes, but what a warm, rich darkness. The grave wasn't in it. No wonder one fought so desperately against being evicted when the nine months lease was up.

ᓚ NATHANAEL WEST

*E*veryone of us needs to be able to escape to a soothing, relaxing place where we can feel whole. Some of us escape to far away places where we can bask in the sun. Some of us escape to the bathroom where we can read the paper in peace. Some of us lie in the grass and daydream, our thoughts drifting with clouds.

What we choose to do is less important than how we feel while we're doing it. If we can tap into the memory of those first accommodations, we will replenish our spirit and rejuvenate our very soul.

Somewhere in my being, I know how to feel nourished and whole.

Discipline comes from the same root as disciple, which means "pupil" or "learner." It suggests that our function as parents is to guide or teach rather than judge.

🖎 LOUISE HART

*I*f we use discipline to force our children to conform to our expectations, hurtful power struggles will ensue. Children will rebel by lashing out or isolating themselves. Either way, they distance themselves from us for their own protection.

While we may see our children as stubborn and spiteful, they are not. They are rebels with a cause, a worthy cause. They are resisting our efforts to make them conform to our wishes. They are fighting for their identity; they are fighting for their very being.

Discipline as control is a misuse of power. Parents who respect their children help them to discover their own uniqueness.

Wrinkles should merely indicate where smiles have been.

           🦋 MARK TWAIN

O ur faces are the road maps of our emotions. Wrinkles mark passages of joy and discovery, surprise and pain, stress and doubt. They give outward expression to our deepest thoughts.

Just as the face is a map, so is the body. The widening of our hips, the length of our stride or the swing of our arms all tell of our struggles and accomplishments, our reticence and indecision, our daring and exploration. Like the annual rings in the trunk of a tree, the marks on our bodies reflect our growth and maturity.

During my lifetime I have traveled many roads— they decorate my face and my body.

*To renew ties with the past need not always be
daydreaming; it may be tapping old sources of
strength for new tasks.*

                     ✒ SIMEON STRUNSKY

O ur past is always accessible to us. The lessons
we learned, the heartaches we endured, the
insights and revelations are all available.

It makes no difference that the scenarios have
changed. The experiences of our past make us who
we are today. Remembering how we made it through
certain trials and when we felt abundant joy are ways
of "tapping old sources of strength for new tasks."

**My past experiences are a source of wisdom from
which I can draw strength.**

The child had every toy his father wanted.

☙ ROBERT E. WHITTEN

*H*aving a child gives all of us an excuse to relive our childhood. For those of us who had sad childhoods, having children provides us with the chance to reinvent our youth.

On one hand, children wear us out. We feel old and haggard. On the other hand, they bring out our youthful exuberance. We buy them the toys we always wanted, and pretty soon, they have to tell *us* to share!

Just because the label reads "Suited for children" doesn't mean that I can't play too!

> *When the snake sheds its skin, it acts as if with instinctual consciousness of rebirth, with acceptance of the process . . . . In contrast to the snake, humanity fears losing the old skin, even when it has begun to constrict our growth.*
>
> VICKI NOBLE

hen we resist our own growth, we suffer. The more tightly we cling to outmoded beliefs and experiences, the more difficult it is to move on to the next phase of our life. Our fear of change constricts our evolution and awareness. We stubbornly insist that "the old skin" fits even though it is coming apart at the seams.

If we could become more like the shedding snake, we would probably discover that growth is less painful than resistance.

Growth leads to renewal. When I am ready, I will shed my old skin.

*God intended motherhood to be a relay race. Each
generation would pass the baton on to the next.
But the baton has been fumbled. So, it's our job—
yours and mine—to pick it up. We have to do more
than follow in our mother's footsteps; we have to . . .
rediscover the lost art of mothering.*

                   MARY PRIDE

The wisdom of motherhood was originally
passed down through the generations. Oral
traditions and maternal mentors initiated women into
this sacred art form.

In today's world, it is not always possible to maintain closeknit families and inter-generational communities. However, by creating our own groups of
dedicated mothers, we can reclaim the art of mothering and pass it on. We can draw strength from the
rich traditions that honor motherhood.

I must learn anew a lost art, and pass on the wisdom of my maternal experience.

We are aware of our hunger and needs, but still ignorant of what will satisfy them.... Not knowing how to feed the spirit, we try to muffle its demands in distractions. Instead of stilling the center, the axis of the wheel, we add more centrifugal activities to our lives—which tend to throw us off balance.

        🖎 ANNE MORROW LINDBERGH

*A*t times, we all feel a spiritual hunger. This is especially true when caring for our new baby leaves us weary and depleted. "Not knowing how to feed the spirit, we try to muffle its demands in distractions." We throw ourselves into activities and causes that pull us further and further from our core. Instead of going inward to the source, we look outside, hoping to find whatever will complete us and make us feel whole.

To replenish our spiritual center, we need to still "the axis of the wheel" and pull ourselves inward.

My spirituality is in here, not out there.

Have the courage to act instead of react.

☙ EARLENE LARSON JENKS

*O*ne of the signs of immaturity exhibited by children is indiscriminate rebellion. To assert their individuality they're against whatever we are for. Many adults act the same way.

When we were children, rebellion served a purpose. We were testing our independence or protecting our self-esteem. However, rebellion can outlive its usefulness. When we have to define ourselves by being against something or someone, we create a negative identity.

Whenever we react to an exising situation, it is usually because we're afraid to make our own choices. We must "have the courage to act instead of react." Re-action wastes the energy we could be using to shape our own lives.

It is easier to find fault with what already is, than to have the courage to create something new.

Arguing

Make sure you never, never argue at night. You just lose a good night's sleep, and you can't settle anything until morning anyway.

                 ❧ ROSE KENNEDY

*P*arents of newborns are notorious for arguing at night. For one thing, we're up for half of it. Although we take turns putting the baby back to sleep, we grumble while we're doing it. If the baby won't fall asleep when it's our turn, we grumble even louder. When our spouse offers to help, we get angry. If he doesn't offer to help, we're furious! As one very tired mother said: "I'm just not my best at 2:00 a.m., and 4:00 a.m., and 6:00 a.m. . . ."

There *is*, however, one advantage to arguing at night. By morning, we probably won't remember what we were arguing about.

I don't want to argue in front of my children. I don't want to argue at night. So, when is a good time to argue?

Courage

*That is at the bottom the only courage that is
demanded of us: to have courage for the most
inexplicable that we may encounter. That mankind
has in this sense been cowardly has done life endless
harm; the experiences that are called "visions,"
the so-called "spirit world," death, all those things
that are so closely akin to us, have by daily parrying
been so crowded out of life that the senses by which we
could have grasped them are atrophied. To say
nothing of God.*

                         ✑ RAINER MARIA RILKE

Why have we been so cowardly? Why have we chosen to close off our senses to those things which are most vital to us?

Visions are reserved for the artists and poets. Even then, if their vision is too consuming, we label them madmen. Yet, our children come into the world without these veils and fears. The "spirit world," God's presence and visions are as real to them as the car parked in the driveway.

Our children can illuminate aspects of reality we might otherwise miss. Because they *see*, they can show us the absurd profundity that is life.

May I have the courage to open my senses to the inexplicable.

For me, motherhood has been the one true, great, and wholly successful romance. It is the only love I have known that is expansive and that could have stretched to contain with equal passion more than one object. . . .

                                   ERMA KURTZ

*B*eing a mother teaches us a great deal about love. We now have the opportunity to feel the expansive nature of love. Love without end.

Our love for our children expands with them, encompassing them without restricting their movement and growth. It is passionate and strong. It is committed and true. We fall deeper in love, making all our relationships more fulfilling, and we renew our romance with life.

To experience the expansive nature of love is one of the best parts of being a mother.

Worry

He makes fuzz come out of my bald patch!
ʖCHARLES A. LINDBERGH

hildren have an uncanny ability to put the fear of God into us. They run into walls, scale the sides of their crib, lean over bathtubs, jump down stairs, and rush toward swimming pools. If we have hair, it falls out. If we have a bald patch, it grows fuzz.

Sure, we want our children to stretch their abilities. (Heaven forbid that we impinge upon their exploration.) We even want them to enjoy themselves. Then why are we such a nervous wreck? Because we watch our little ones come within inches of their life, daily. They think it's funny. We smile weakly and try not to pull out our hair.

As comedian Damon Wayans put it, "I'm 29, but I've got three kids. That makes me 29 to the fifth power!" And the numbers are multiplying....

Years may wrinkle the skin. Lack of enthusiasm will wrinkle the soul.

ANONYMOUS

I once read that the word "enthusiasm" means "the God within." Makes sense, doesn't it?

Whenever we lack enthusiasm, life is without passion. We feel disconnected from ourselves, cut off from our spiritual centers. We probably lack focus and direction, not because we're in the midst of a transition, but because we've entered a state of non-living. We conduct the rituals of our lives out of duty, not out of enthusiasm.

Where has our hope gone? When did we deaden ourselves to life? How long has it been since we've communicated with "the God within?" Maybe it's time we had a talk.

To be enthusiastic about life, I must fully choose to live it.

Do not mistake a child for his symptoms.

❧ ERIK ERIKSON

*T*oo often, we label children prematurely. We formulate opinions about who they are based on transitory behavior. "He's stubborn." "She's slow." "He's aggressive." "She's timid." If we're not careful, we can create a self-fulfilling prophecy. Instead of passing through a phase of growth, our child will continue to exhibit the behaviors we attributed to him.

Unless we can separate our child from his behavior, we will never know who he really is. We will continue to relate to his symptoms instead of his self. How can we expect him to change when our labels have already condemned him to our limited perception?

If I mistake my child for his behavior, I miss out on who he really is.

A man is not idle because he is absorbed in thought.
There is a visible labor and there is an invisible labor.
                             VICTOR HUGO

*E*very one of us needs time to reflect—to sort
things out, think them through. Focusing
on what we want, and knowing what really matters
to us, is just as important as taking steps toward our
goals. If we do not allow ourselves time to "labor
invisibly," we will not be clear about our choices. We
will forge ahead, slightly off course. And maybe never
know where we are or where we're headed.

**Getting clear about where I'm going helps me to
get there.**

It took me a while to deal with the grief and disappointment I felt after delivering by c-section because everyone kept saying, "It doesn't matter as long as you've had a healthy baby."

                     ✍ ANONYMOUS MOTHER

Grief is a common feeling among women who deliver by caesarean—as well as a sense of failure. We feel we've missed our chance to experience a "real" birth. We feel we gave our child less than the best introduction to life.

We question ourselves: "Could I have done anything to prevent surgery?" "Why couldn't I have a natural birth like other mothers?"

As we accept our grief, we begin to heal, although we may not know exactly why things happened the way they did. What is important is that we come to terms with our feelings and that we see them as legitimate.

Having a healthy baby helps me to deal with my grief, but it does not completely remove it—only I can do that.

Educate a man and you educate an individual—
educate a woman and you educate a family.

AGNES CRIPPS

others are teachers. Whatever we learn, whatever knowledge we possess, we impart to our children. To a large degree, we determine what our children will grow up knowing about themselves and their world.

Despite the added stress of working outside the home, we still manage to educate our children. As my husband once told me: "By the time men return home from work, they've used up their 15,000 words for the day. Women, being more verbal, have about 10,000 words left to use." What do we do with these "extra words"? Teach.

"It is a greater work to educate a child," William Channing once wrote, **"than to rule a state."**

It is the friends you can call up at 4:00 a.m. that matter.

                 ❧ MARLENE DIETRICH

*E*veryone of us needs to have special friends. People with whom we can share our insights and confusion. People we can count on and trust. At no time is this more necessary than when we have a baby.

Of all the gifts we receive, the most meaningful ones are those that come from the heart. The friends who bring us breakfast because we are too weak to get up; the friends who run the vacuum and wash the dishes; the friends we can call at 4:00 a.m. These are the friends who really matter.

Friends give the gift of their time. They share who they are with us. They know without our having to tell them what is in our heart.

I cherish my friendships. They give me sustenance and strength, laughter and joy.

Nothing feeds the center more than creative work, even humble kinds like cooking and sewing.

 ANNE MORROW LINDBERGH

*W*hen we think of creative work, we usually think of it on a grand scale. We overlook the everyday creative tasks because they have become one more chore on a long list of chores. When we cram them into an already overcrowded schedule, they cease to be contemplative activities. Rather than "feeding the center," they threaten to consume us.

Perhaps, as Mrs. Lindbergh says, "Nothing feeds the center more than creative work...." We need to find a sense of fulfillment in the simple things. We need to take time to be inwardly attentive.

If I do not feed my center with creative work, it will dry up and crack like the earth in a drought.

Aim for success, not perfection. Never give up your right to be wrong, because then you will lose the ability to learn new things and move forward with your life. Remember that fear always lurks behind perfectionism.

🌀 DR. DAVID M. BURNS

*O*ne of the most important things mothers can do for their children is to value themselves. To do this, we must stop comparing ourselves in competitive ways. Comparison affects our self-esteem—usually by lowering it—and traps us in a cycle of perfectionism. We never measure up. We feel inadequate and we obsess over our shortcomings.

When we don't value ourselves, we tend to expect too much of those around us. We're more critical of what others do and say. In short, we're treating others in the same way we are treating ourselves—as if they should be perfect.

Being successful is not the same as being perfect. It allows me to value myself, even when I am wrong.

. . . the decline of the extended family creates the need for a new social shelter, another pool of friendships, another bond with society apart from the family.

        ☙ ARLIE HOCHSCHILD

*M*any of us are separated from close friends and family. We've moved to another state, our family has been dispersed around the country, or everyone is just too busy to help out. Whatever the scenario, we find ourselves isolated with our child. We need support, yet we don't know where to turn. We are mothers without a community.

Today, more than ever, mothers need to find "a new social shelter." We need to form bonds with others who can provide support and friendship. But where do we look? Adult education classes, co-op babysitting groups, playgroups, birthing classes, preschools, churches—all of these networks can put us in touch with others who share our need for, and commitment to, community.

I need to extend beyond my family. I can create my own community of support.

I may have faults but being wrong ain't one of them.
              ❧ JIMMY HOFFA

*A*dmitting we are wrong is not easy. We fear that the image others hold of us might be altered or damaged.

Self-righteousness is a form of stubbornness. It is a symptom of perfectionism that precludes us from learning from our mistakes. Always needing to be right, we close ourselves off from new knowledge. How can we learn from experience when we already know everything? How can we grow and move forward with our lives when a disproportionate amount of energy goes into saving appearances?

The funny thing is, we're the only ones who refuse to see our mistakes. They're apparent to those around us, and if we'd only own up to them, others wouldn't care so much about our foibles.

Wouldn't it be wiser to admit my mistakes than to be trapped in the stagnation of self-righteousness?

One of the advantages of being disorderly is that one is constantly making exciting discoveries.

                A. A. MILNE

No matter how much housework we manage to get done, there's always something left to do. Although we cannot always control the growth of disorderly mess, we can change our attitude. Like our children, we can consider the unsightly things we come across as buried treasure. Whenever a soggy baby's bib turns up in the stack of dirty dishes, we can think of it as a discovery.

While there may not be many advantages to being disorderly, there is one—we are "constantly making new discoveries."

If I can manage to keep a humorous attitude, I can better manage my life as a mother.

Humor is the affectionate communication of insight.
ॐ LEO ROSTEN

W hen we share our parenting anecdotes with others, it adds color to our lives. Not only that, but we see them in a new light.

Humor has a way of magnifying universal truths. It gives us perspective—suddenly we can see the absurdity in a situation that, at the time, we thought was a major crisis. Laughing with another first-time parent who made the same fumbling mistakes, means we don't take ourselves or our parenting quite so seriously. We realize that others struggle with the same things, as we do, and we don't feel so alone.

**Just knowing I'm not the *only* one who broke
a breast pump, couldn't unfold the stroller, etc.,
makes me feel better.**

I'm consistently inconsistent.

🖎 ELIZABETH YARDLEY

*W*hen we are inconsistent, our children learn that they cannot rely on us. Our word is no good. The only thing that they can count on is our inconsistency. The rules change according to our moods and whims. Our children feel insecure because they never know what our response will be.

When we are consistent, we keep our promises. We are true to our word. Our children know we will not betray them. We are flexible in our responses because we realize that there are exceptions to any rules.

Being consistent about the important things is what matters. It helps us to build long-lasting trust and mutual respect.

Consistency builds a relationship of trust with my children.

*When you're hovering at the edge of an abyss, it
doesn't take much to push you over.*

CINDY GRISWOLD

The stress of motherhood pushes us to the
brink. We teeter back and forth, hoping not to
fall over the edge. We're operating on a survival
mode, barely holding things together. One unexpected change can throw off the delicate balance
we've tried so hard to achieve.

Perhaps the most frustrating aspect of this real life
scenario is that change is slow. Relief is temporary.
Unless we want to traumatize our children, changes
must be done gradually, over time.

Hopefully, the insanity of the situation will be the
catalyst for more sweeping changes in our lifestyle.
Until then, we learn to jump back from the abyss,
even if we're only landing on the edge.

**Teetering on the edge is an unavoidable aspect
of new motherhood. But do I have to make a lifestyle out of it?**

Laughter can be more satisfying than honor; more precious than money; more heart-cleansing than prayer.

        ❧ HARRIET ROCHLIN

*L*aughter is like inner jogging. Not only does it exercise our facial muscles, but it also releases tension. It reminds us to breathe deeply. When we laugh, anger fades, our perspective changes. We turn serious questions on their heads. Yes, yes, yes, laughter feels so good! To let go a deep belly-laugh and hear the sound of our voice reverberating off the walls—there's nothing like it.

For those of us who need it, there's even proof that laughter is healthy: scientific studies claim that the very act of smiling releases endorphins, the "happy hormones," into the body. Even those of us who laugh self-consciously can't help but benefit from the eruption. Laughter keeps me healthy because it keeps me sane.

A good laugh is as cleansing as a good cry.

Affirmation of life is the spiritual act by which man ceases to live unreflectively and begins to devote himself to his life with reverence in order to raise it to its true value. To affirm life is to deepen, to make more inward, and to exalt the will to live.

ALBERT SCHWEITZER

*G*iving birth is an affirmation of life. It is a spiritual act that deepens us, and brings us closer to the source. Like other significant moments, childbirth reaffirms our sacred connection to life and helps us to "raise it to its true value."

From that moment on, relationships take on a different light and we become more conscious of our relationship to a larger whole. As new mothers, we are no longer observers, but participants in the flow of life. We "exalt the will to live."

The more I affirm life, the more fully I live.

. . . I could feel in my soul the acute longing for someone to mother me.

🐌 MELINDA BURNS

How many of us have felt the same way? We long to have someone take care of us for a while; someone to tell us, "Honey, you're tired. It's time to go to sleep." We long to have our hair stroked, to be taken on a magical journey where we float on imaginary pink clouds. We long to feel the soothing touch that only a mother can provide, to be told that everything is going to be O.K.

When we feel this longing, it is the child within telling us that she, too, needs to be nurtured. She needs to be held and cuddled, just as our own child does. The child within needs a lap.

The need for nurturing and loving attention is not reserved for children. I, too, need it.

I believe in the power that created the universe. I pray every morning. My prayers consist of one word: HELP. That's it—over and out. And then I get up and do something.

           ✍ SAM MEIER (SERENITY SAM)

Mothers live complicated lives. Why, then, do we complicate them further by insisting on lengthy prayers? We think we have to pray in a certain way and feel guilty if we don't "pray right." There are so many items on our agenda that we don't know where to start. After a while, praying becomes too burdensome. It feels like reciting a lengthy lesson. The result is that we stop praying.

There is another option: Keep It Simple.

When it comes to prayer, the unspoken words are just as powerful as the spoken ones.

Keeping house is like threading beads on a string with no knot at the end.

🖎 ANONYMOUS

*W*e go to great lengths to set our proverbial house in order, only to discover that "there's no knot at the end of the string." Things keep running together whether we want them to or not. We may delude ourselves into thinking that we can tidy up all the loose ends, but at some point we realize that the various aspects of our lives bleed together like a watercolor painting. Inevitably, any order we impose breaks down, and we discover that order is as arbitrary as the borders surrounding a country.

Life is never static. As Betty Talmadge says: "Life is what happens to you when you're making other plans."

If I'm not careful, I'll miss life while making other plans.

Dreams say what they mean, but they don't say it in daytime language.

GAIL GOODWIN

Dream life for pregnant women and women who have newly given birth is full, as full as we feel. Dreams help us to integrate the feelings we have about becoming a mother. They may reflect our fears or mirror our desires about the kind of mother we would like to be.

Dreams serve many purposes. Threatening dreams in which we are attacked may speak to our maternal instincts. Do we feel capable of protecting our child? Serene dreams put us in touch with the essence of motherhood. They help us to feel comfortable in our nurturing role. And bizarre dreams may simply be indigestion.

The language of dreams has many different dialects. If I listen closely, I can decipher their meaning.

A single event can awaken within us a stranger totally unknown to us. To live is to be slowly born.
                              ANTOINE DE SAINT-EXUPERY

*T*he events that transform us stay fresh in our minds. They take us deeper into ourselves; they move us into a new level of existence; they excavate our souls.

Giving birth is one of the most transformative experiences we can have. This single event "awakens within us a stranger totally unknown to us." We bring new life into the world, and by so doing, breathe new life into ourselves.

The events of life give me the opportunity to be born again and again and again. I am made anew.

*They had no serenity, for true serenity comes after
knowledge of pain. They had only the stillness of
spiritual inertia. They were half alive.*

🐾 MARYA MANNES

*P*ain can be a powerful teacher. However,
when we do not learn from our pain, we
stunt our own growth. By holding onto it, we
become identified with our pain. Like unworked clay,
it hardens, calcifying the mind and heart.

When we accumulate enough hurt, pain becomes
a deadening force. The stillness we experience does
not come from serenity but from inertia. We are only
half alive. Serenity seems distant and unattainable.

**When I begin to feel and know my pain, it softens
in the same way that clay softens when it is
touched by warm hands.**

Love

The baby is practicing loving for life. The more he can love, now, and feel himself loved back, the more generous with, and accepting of, all kinds of love he will be, right through his life.

🌿 PENELOPE LEACH

*I*f we are stingy with our love, our child learns that love is scarce and becomes needy. If we are generous with our love, she learns the abundance of love and gives it unconditionally. If we use love as a weapon and give it only when we approve of our child's actions, then she learns how to manipulate, not how to love. If we give love indiscriminately, our child does not learn about personal boundaries and needlessly gives herself away.

We are laying lifelong foundations for loving. There are no dry-runs, no practice sessions. This is it. Through our love, we teach our child to love. And how we love is just as important as how much we love.

How do I like to be loved? Can I love my child in the same way?

She seems to have had the ability to stand firmly on the rock of her past while living completely and unregretfully in the present.

     ❧ MADELEINE L'ENGLE

*E*ach of us knows someone like this; someone who is comfortable with herself because she knows who she is. Someone who has integrated her past into who she is today.

Once we incorporate our social, ethnic, and intellectual background into who we are today, we can embrace our journey completely. All that we are and all that we have been come together. We unite our various selves.

That doesn't mean we wouldn't do some things differently. But it does mean that we carry the wisdom we earned with us and live without regrets.

My past need not weigh me down; it can anchor me in the present.

*Your children need your presence more than they need
your presents.*

🍼 JESSE JACKSON

*A*dding motherhood to a career puts a lot on
our plates. If we become fully absorbed in
our work, we are inaccessible to those we love.

Feeling guilty is useless. What we need to do is
make concrete changes. For some women, the solution lies in becoming "downwardly mobile." For
some of us, writes Jane McCormick White in *Mothering Magazine,* the solution lies in giving up high
stress/high paid jobs in exchange for more time with
family. The time spent supporting a glamorous lifestyle is time we'd rather spend with our children.
Others of us start our own businesses so we can better manage our schedules. Still others choose to work
part-time.

Without question, our careers are important to
us. They are a symbol of our gifts and talents. However, knowing when the price is too high is essential
to our own and our children's well-being.

**I need to remember that my career decisions affect
my children.**

There was no use in apologizing for the way I looked. Nobody looked the way I did who expected to be seen by anyone else.

🌿 AGNES DE MILLE

By the time the second child arrives, we stop apologizing. But for first-time mothers, it's a different story. We're so silly about how we look! We forget that our lives are not a Hollywood movie where the heroine gives birth in five minutes, and looks stunningly gorgeous afterwards—not a hair out of place! We're regular people who are too tired to put on makeup, and may not be able to shower until baby takes a nap. When's the last time we had the leisure to look in a mirror? At least for a while, we live in our robes, shuffling around the house in our slippers, and we shop at night. We don't expect to be seen by anyone else.

I don't expect a triathlete to be neat and tidy after a race. Why should I expect any more of myself?

Once Eleza was doing more than merely screaming or sleeping, I wanted to talk endlessly about our adorable and clever little petunia blossom. Who else was as interested in her as I? Who else but my husband could appreciate the subtle changes that go unobserved by all others?

❧ CAROL KORT

When we enter into motherhood, we enter into a new world. We become totally absorbed in our little microcosm and totally entranced with our infant. Try as we might, we can't always communicate all the subtle changes that take place each day in our child. Sometimes we can't find the words; at other times, our friends may not be able to relate to our experience. It is as if we are living in parallel universes.

Our children have opened up a new dimension of life for us. We want to include others in our discovery. But as a close friend once told me, "When you change, you want to take everyone with you on your new journey, but they may not be packed! In fact, they may be on an entirely different flight!"

I will tell my joy to those who can share and appreciate the journey into motherhood.

Motherhood brings as much joy as ever, but it still brings boredom, exhaustion, and sorrow too. Nothing else will ever make you as happy or as sad, as proud or as tired, for nothing is quite as hard as helping a person develop his own individuality—especially while you struggle to keep your own.

         ✍ MARGUERITE KELLY AND ELIA PARSONS

aintaining our individuality is one of the most challenging aspects of motherhood. Our children inhabit a part of us. An invisible umbilical cord joins us, and although the cord stretches and thins with each move toward independence, we feel its tugging. We want to encourage our children to become individuals without becoming a beacon for their souls. Is it any wonder why such a task may occasionally rearrange our personal boundaries? We give so much of ourselves that we must be careful not to give ourselves away.

Maintaining my own individuality helps my child to develop a stronger sense of self. We both benefit.

Chaos often breeds life, when order breeds habit.
%& HENRY ADAMS

C haos can shake us loose from our habits, forcing us to consider new options. Whenever we have been lulled into a false sense of security, chaos abruptly sheds light on the reality of the situation.

However, continual chaos wears us down. Our senses become overwhelmed and we feel confused. Unsheathed, we are susceptible to giving in when we don't really want to. It is hard to maintain our center.

Chaos often breeds life. But too much chaos breeds destruction.

A mother understands what a child does not say.
     ॐ JEWISH PROVERB

*M*others are proficient in nonverbal communication. We listen with an inner ear. We hear our child even in the midst of silence. We hear the words our child cannot say.

Whenever others correct us, saying, "He's not tired," "He's not hungry," "You're only imagining what he thinks," we know better. We know the language of our own child. We are tuned in to his cues and his expressions, and what they mean. We understand the mystical language that takes place between mothers and their children.

With infants, nonverbal communication is infinitely more important than the spoken word.

*Experience is not what happens to you. It is what you
do with what happens to you.*

> 🐾 ALDOUS HUXLEY

A friend recently gave me an article about
"transcenders": individuals who flourish
despite traumatic childhoods. The main question the
researchers asked: "What makes these children different from those who are crushed by their upbring-
ing?" The answer seemed so simple to me: it's what
they do with what's happened to them that makes
them so successful. When life gives them lemons,
they make lemonade.

We all have the ability to transcend the bad events
in our lives. We do this when we trust our own perceptions about our childhood. By acknowledging
what frightened and wounded us as children, we're
more prepared to protect our child. And realizing that
we are now the adults enables us to change a bad
situation instead of having to adjust to it as children
often must.

**My past need not determine what kind of a mother
I am.**

The Value of Time

What is the price of an afternoon when a small girl is soothed in your arms, when the sun bolts through a doorway and both you and the child are very young?
❧ DOROTHY EVSLIN

In our utilitarian society, time is always to be used, never to be wasted. Is it any wonder why we always feel pressure to be doing something? To be moving toward some future goal? But what does it mean to make good use of time?

We think of time in limited terms; there's never enough of it. Yet, time, by its nature, is infinite. When we slow down to a more natural rhythm, allowing ourselves to absorb the richness of the mothering experience, time becomes inconsequential. By living fully in the moment, we suspend time and savor the moment.

Thinking of time in terms of scarcity only restricts my experience of it. A moment in time can be infinite.

Complaining

It's easy to complain about children. But when we want to express our joy, our love, the words elude us. The feelings are almost so sacred they defy speech.

                         ♫ JOAN MCINTOSH

We often hear people complaining about their children. We complain about our own children. Granted, we may qualify our complaints with phrases like "I love my child, but . . ." "It's not that he's a bad kid, but . . ." The fact is, it's easier to complain. Complaints aren't threatening. Our more intimate feelings are, however.

Sometimes if we express the feelings that are closest to our hearts, others become uneasy. When we sense their discomfort, we feel inhibited. Fortunately, there are those close to us who listen patiently as we struggle to verbalize the richness of our experience with our children.

If the words elude me, maybe it is better to remain quiet, than to resort to complaining.

Being a mother, as far as I can tell, is a constantly evolving process of adapting to the needs of your child while also changing and growing as a person in your own right.

🖎 DEBORAH INSEL

*N*ot so long ago, being a mother meant giving up one's own identity, or at least submerging it for the needs of the child. Fortunately, we have acquired a more balanced view. We now realize that children benefit from a mother who continues to grow alongside them. Although we continue to adapt to the needs of our children, we do not ignore our own yearnings. Although we continue to make sacrifices, we do not sacrifice ourselves.

When I remain a person in my own right, I am less likely to look to my children to define me.

Any adult who spends even fifteen minutes with a child outdoors finds himself drawn back to his own childhood, like Alice falling down the rabbit hole.
❧ SHARON MACLATCHIE

Many of us go through periods when we only remember the anguish and turmoil of our childhood. Although this is a necessary part of purging our pain, it need not be a permanent place of residence.

When we are ready, we can follow our children outdoors. We can share their intense fascination with the smallest details of a flower; the spots on a ladybug's back; the strands of a spider's web. With them, we can be drawn back to the magic of our own childhood. We can "fall down the rabbit hole" and discover the treasures of childhood that have been buried deep in our hearts.

Like nature, children have a healing influence on my life.

Insanity is hereditary—you get it from your kids.
℘ SAM LEVINSON

*W*hat is it about kids that makes us crazy? Could it be the way they whine? Or the way they run out into the street? Maybe it's just their knack for doing things they shouldn't do—you know, those annoying little things that could easily end their life!

When we try to keep them safe, they feel restricted. When we try not to interfere, they feel ignored. When we try to set reasonable limits, they push us to our limit. As the comedian, Sinbad, describes it: "You used to be normal. Then you have kids and you spend the rest of your life yelling at something you don't understand!"

To quote Shakespeare: "Though this be madness, there be method in't."

Sharing the Burden

Men who shared the load at home seemed just as pressed for time as their wives, and torn between the demands of career and small children.... But the majority of men did not share the load at home. Some refused outright. Others refused more passively, often offering a loving shoulder to lean on, an understanding ear as their working wife faced the conflict they both saw as hers.

🖐 ARLIE HOCHSCHILD

*H*ow many of us struggle to balance motherhood with a career? How many of us feel torn by the demands of small children, as though our work life and home life are at odds with each other? How many of us feel alone in our struggle and that the problems we face belong solely to us?

Many of us have husbands who give verbal support, but the concrete support we really need rarely materializes. The conflict is seen as ours. They see it as ours, and we see it as ours. Until the problem belongs to both of us, things will remain the same.

Struggling alone with a joint conflict leaves me feeling hollow inside. I need to share the burden of childrearing with my husband.

263

To be successful, the first thing to do is fall in love with your work.

🥀 SISTER MARY LAURETTA

*T*hose of us who based our career choice solely on market forces, often find our work unfulfilling. Our true talents stagnate and our creative energies fade. When we take time off to have children, we may realize how hollow our work lives were.

Sadly, we live in a culture that encourages us to orient ourselves to what will sell. Only "dreamers" follow their vision; only "special" people can create their own careers. Instead of being encouraged to do what we love, we are encouraged to make money, earn a title, or simply feel lucky that we are employed. But what is success if we do not enjoy what we do?

I will choose work that I love—whether at home or in the workplace. Only then will I be successful.

If evolution really works, how come mothers only have two hands?

                    ❧ ED DUSSAULT

*M*others are designed remarkably well. We are capable of doing many things at once. With only two hands, we manage to hold, feed, and clothe an infant while talking on the phone or writing out a check. We perform many functions with the limited apparatus nature has given us.

Just think, if we hadn't adapted, evolution would probably have provided us with ten of everything! It isn't clear whether we'd be more efficient, but we'd definitely be a lot less attractive!

Maybe Mother Nature really knows what she's doing—she's a mother, after all.

...as the life style of the Space Age grows more interdisciplinary, it will be harder and harder for the "one-track" mind to survive...I see simultaneous intake, multiple-awareness, and synthesized comprehension as inevitable, long before the year 2000.

🖋️ BARBARA MORGAN

In other words, the whole world will have to function the same way mothers have been functioning for eons. Everyone, if they are to flourish, will have to acquire what Mary Catherine Bateson calls peripheral vision: "the ability to be attentive to multiple demands; to think about more than one thing at a time."

Instead of becoming "a jack of all trades, good at none," we will have a more sophisticated view, a multi-level awareness of how our actions ripple outward like a stone thrown in a pond. The elaborate juggling acts mothers know so well—the ones that take a broad spectrum of people's needs into account—are the order of the day.

Mothers understand the need for multiple-awareness, and as the world grows more complex, I will continue to broaden my vision.

Nothing is more despicable than respect based on fear.
ALBERT CAMUS

Some of us came from families that more closely resembled a totalitarian state than a loving circle of individuals. Our parents violently demanded our love and respect, and they received neither. Instead, we learned to survive. We learned to be agreeable whenever it was necessary. We learned to avoid conflict. We learned the rules of fear.

Now, with our own children, we have the opportunity to cultivate genuine respect by showing love for our family.

Using fear as a weapon breeds hatred, not respect. I am thankful for the chance to start over with my own children.

═══

*"Look!" my mother and my aunts would cry out to
each baby in turn as it shook a rattle, stood up, peed
in a pot, took the cover off a box and fitted it on
again: "Look"—in joyous amazement, as if such a
thing had never been seen before—"what the baby can
do!"*

                        ✑ DOROTHY DINNERSTEIN

*C*hildren personify the animated intelligence of
the universe. They bring it into focus. They
open our eyes to the extraordinary. With each new
endeavor, they remind us how precious and remarkable it is to be alive. They are a microcosm of the vast
wonders existing all around us. Their small bodies
illuminate the mysteries of the cosmos. Why else
would we cry out in joyous amazement, at each new
accomplishment "as if such a thing had never been
seen before?"

**My children open my awareness to the miracle of
the universe. I am in awe.**

═══

Some problems are just too complicated for rational, logical solutions. They admit of insights, not answers.
              🖘 JEROME WILSNER

*T*he problems of motherhood are frequently "too complicated for rational, logical solutions." The issues are complex, and there is always more than one answer.

The job of motherhood "admits of insights." We cling to answers only when we're unsure of what to do next. If we're afraid to wait for the real answer to emerge, we hastily jump to logical conclusions. We choose to act in a way that is "right," not true. Granted, insights sometimes take longer to enter our consciousness (or, perhaps, our consciousness takes more time to become aware of our insights), but when they do come, they're usually right on the mark.

The insight I need will be revealed when I stop looking for the "right answer."

... The hardest of all is learning to be a well of affection and not a fountain, to show them that we love them, not when we feel like it, but when they do.

NAN FAIRBROTHER

*I*t doesn't take much to get into a "lovefest" with an infant. We kiss his little neck and apple cheeks, caught up in the bliss of motherhood. Then, one day, it happens. Our child flatly says, "No!" and he pulls away from our tender advances.

It's probably the first time it has occurred to us that he is a separate entity. He has boundaries, just as we do, and wants to have a say in what happens to his body. Although we want to continue to shower him with love and affection, we must respect his moods and temperament. We must learn "to show them we love them, not when we feel like it, but when they do."

A vital part of my child's autonomy is knowing he has control of his own body. He should also know my love is always available to him.

Who can refute a sneer?

❧ WILLIAM PALEY

While I was visiting relatives in Canada, my uncle told a joke: Before you're married, you have sex all over the place—on the kitchen floor, in the living room, even in the tub. When you get married, you have "bedroom sex." After you have children, you have "hallway sex." You pass each other in the hallway and say, "Screw you!"

The stress of having children can put us at each other's throats. We both feel we're giving our all and we take our frustrations out on each other.

Instead of exchanging harsh words, why don't we try a sneer? If we contort our faces into the gargoyles we feel we've become, we might get a smile, and then we can both have a good laugh at ourselves.

Perhaps if I exaggerate how I feel, I'll rediscover my sense of humor.

Fear ringed by doubt is my eternal moon.

🐚 MALCOLM LOWRY

*I*nevitably, most of us will have to face an unforeseen illness or emergency that affects our child. When it happens, our fear will be ringed by doubt. Was there a way to prevent this? Who's responsible? Am I to blame?

Those of us who give birth prematurely learn early what it is like to fear for our child's life. We were thrown into a situation where we had to depend on outside authorities to care for our baby. We felt help-less and frightened, filled with doubt. Am I receiving the best help possible? Is there anyting I can do for my child? How can they be sure they're doing the right thing? Our agony felt as eternal as the moon.

When our baby recovers, we almost can't believe it's true. The rest of the world seems to have disap-peared. Our hope and faith feel badly shaken. Like our infant, we, too, will need time to heal and mend our hearts.

Crisis holds me hostage to fear. I need the support and assurance of others to help negotiate my release.

Cats seem to go on the principle that it never does any harm to ask for what you want.

❧ JOSEPH WOOD KRUTCH

*B*abies seem to go on the same principle.
When they're newborns, asking for what they want comes in the form of a cry. Later, their repertoire expands. They point, grunt, scream, grab. Sometimes our child can't decide what he wants and we trip all over ourselves trying to help him figure it out.

The same is true for mothers. When we're consistently overwhelmed by simple choices and decisions, it's a sign that we need to relax. We need to take time to figure out what we want. A babysitter? Time alone? A hot shower? It never hurts to ask. . .

I need to know what I want before I can ask for it.

Our third child changed our lives dramatically. It was the first time we were outnumbered.

                   ✑ TOM AND LESLIE MCCLURE

*P*arents can only stretch so far. We have only so many eyes, arms and legs. And there are only two of us.

It's slightly unnerving when our children outnumber us. Although we want them to be close friends, we're a little afraid that they might conspire against us; wage war; plot a rebellion. Our resources are spread so thin that they'd have no difficulty wiping us out. Knowing this makes us sleep with one eye open.

However, there is one advantage to having more than two children: it draws us closer together. If not for reasons of love, then for reasons of survival!

Nothing unites a team more than being outnumbered.

Healthy children will not fear life if their elders have integrity enough not to fear death.

👉 ERIK ERIKSON

*D*eath is feared in our culture. It is seen as an ending, rather than a natural part of life. We go to great lengths to avoid death and miss out on living our lives. We escape into addictions, deny our spirituality, and resist inner growth. Could it be that we fear living as much as we fear death?

Certainly, to be fully alive takes a great deal of courage. We must be open to the unknown, and in so doing, we come to know it. We confront the deeper aspects of ourselves, and we are initiated into "The Great Mystery." We embrace death as an aspect of life, and fear it no more.

If my children learn to see death as a culmination of a life well-lived, they will not be afraid to live life fully.

To bring up a child in the way he should go, travel that way yourself once in a while.

JOSH BILLINGS

We all want to set a good example for our children. Yet, many of us get caught in the trap of perfectionism. If we are not perfect role models, we fear that our children won't respect us. What we forget is that a perfect person is hard to live up to.

Instead, we could travel the path of humanness. Instead of telling our children that a good person is a perfect person, we could show them that there are many different kinds of wonderful people. Instead of telling them that they should act in a perfect way, we could show them the road to travel, even when we occasionally go astray.

To be a healthy role model for my children, I should admit to them that I, like everyone else, am not perfect.

*There are no limits to God's compassion with
Paradises over their one, universally felt want; he
immediately created other animals besides. God's first
blunder: Man didn't find the animals amusing—he
dominated them, and didn't even want to be an
"animal."*

        ♏ FRIEDRICH NIETZSCHE

"Never trust anyone who is cruel to an animal," my grandfather once told me. "If he
doesn't have compassion for creatures who depend
on his goodwill for their survival, he doesn't hold an
adequate reverence for life."

In many cultures, animals are thought of as relatives
and people value the interconnectedness of life. They
realize that if we separate ourselves and try to dominate the animal kingdom, we contribute to our own
demise.

Whenever we see ourselves as superior to animals
and children, we miss out on the extraordinary things
they have to teach us. Whenever we do not treat
them with dignity, we divorce ourselves from the
world family and our spirit suffers.

**Everything that lives is holy. When I open myself
to children and animals, I am humbled by the
extent of their wisdom.**

*I felt that blank incapability of invention which is
the greatest misery of authorship, when dull Nothing
replies to our anxious invocations.*

🖐 MARY SHELLEY

*J*t takes energy to creatively respond to the
needs of our baby. But creativity cannot always
be summoned on demand. It has its own cadence
and rhythm. Some days the muse eludes us. At other
times, we feel like an open channel for the muse.

Motherhood has an ebb and flow. Some days we
feel stilted, bound by monotony. On other days, we
fill our hours with creative adventures and effortless
play. On those mornings when only "dull Nothing
replies," we feel like a novelist with writer's block.
The more we wish this blank feeling would go away,
the stronger it seems to envelop us. All we can do is
be with the feeling until our creative energy returns
and carries us forward.

**Just like artists, mothers get stuck from time to
time.**

I wish the first year had been easier for me, but then I realize that if it had been easier, I would have been raising a different child, and I love my child.

              🌿 ANONYMOUS

A "high need" child is not easy to deal with, especially when it is our first child. They usually cry more than most children, or refuse to be put down, or take a bottle. They like to suck at the breast long after they are full. They don't take regular naps, they "catnap." Their behavior creates a lot more work and aggravation.

When we try to explain our situation to parents with "easier" babies, they can't empathize. At best, they think we're exaggerating. If we don't receive support for our special predicament, we begin to wonder if something *is* wrong with us. Finally, when we discover books and articles that accurately describe the characteristics of our infant, we feel relieved. "High need" babies do exist, and so do their mothers.

Having a "high need" baby means I have more demands placed on me. I am not alone, although I often feel all alone.

No one worth possessing can quite be possessed.
             ❧ SARA TEASDALE

Not so long ago, children were legally considered property. As property, they had no rights. Today, our laws protect children.

However, laws cannot always change attitudes. We may not see ourselves as parents who treat their children like property, but maybe we are. Do we respect our children's feelings and moods? Are we atuned to their wants and needs? Do we see our children as extensions of ourselves, or as human beings with rights?

When we truly respect our children we know that they are too valuable to possess. And, through our actions, we illustrate our deep gratitude for their presence.

Children are not our possessions. We are entrusted with their care.

A great part of courage is the courage of having done the thing before.

🖎 RALPH WALDO EMERSON

Giving birth for the first time takes courage, trust and faith. We dive into the unknown. We don't know what will happen or what to expect.

Unfortunately, for some of us, our first birthing experience was rough. The pain was unbearable, our body was invaded with medical instruments, our belly was hurriedly cut open, and we were at the mercy of gruff, callous doctors and nurses. We felt joy at the sight of our baby; our body and spirit felt pummeled. Could we ever go through this again? We doubted it.

For months, perhaps years, we try to reconcile the conflicting feelings associated with childbirth. Over and over, we review the details of what happened. We know the variables. They have taught us how we might do it differently the next time. Slowly, if we give ourselves time to heal, our courage returns.

Knowing I survived the first time helps me to have the courage to give birth again. Hopefully, things will be better the second time around.

There are few human beings who receive the truth, complete and staggering, by instant illumination. Most of them acquire it fragment by fragment, on a small scale, by successive developments, all wearily, like a laborious mosaic.

🍃 ANAIS NIN

*E*nlightenment usually comes with time, and it's a good thing, too. Just think how boring life would be if we knew everything there was to know. How dull it would be to be a "fully realized" human being. The things we'd miss . . . .

As my father always says, "There's no substitute for direct experience." Slowly we put the pieces of experience together, making important connections that magnify truth. We may never complete "the laborious mosaic" but that is not what matters. That our experiences increase our awareness and animate our consciousness—that is what makes life worth living.

As my life unfolds, it brings many gifts and treasures. I am dazzled by the small daily illuminations.

What does not destroy me, makes me strong.

          ❧ NIETZSCHE

*C*hildren test a marriage—any marriage. Yet children do not destroy a marriage. Without a sound foundation a marriage will crumble under the strain or explode under the pressure.

In the long run, dissolution of an unstable marriage is usually a blessing in disguise. Yet when we are in the midst of separating from our spouse, it is a wrenching and heartbreaking experience. We feel like failures, ashamed that we cannot sustain a long-term partnership. We blame ourselves for whatever went wrong.

Divorce feels so final, as we go through it. However, if we can see it as a transition, albeit a painful and complicated transition, divorce can be a beginning: the beginning of a new life for ourselves and our children.

Explosions can shatter us. They can also cleanse us and make us strong.

Delusions of Adequacy

You're obviously suffering from delusions of adequacy.

🖜 ALEXIS CARRINGTON

A father of a six-year-old daughter and I were discussing the challenge of keeping up with our children. We talked about being sensitive to their needs and being aware of their struggles. Then, he confided: "You know, just when I thought I was getting really good at this parenting stuff, a new situation came up, and I felt totally inadequate!"

Sometimes we act as if parenting is like installing a car battery; once we learn how to do it, it's always done the same way. Parenting is the opposite. Once we learn how to do it, we can be assured that we'll have to learn how to do it again (and again, and again). Modification and alteration are a way of life. Fortunately, it's not a bad way of life.

If ever I'm suffering from delusions of adequacy, my children will find a cure.

You know the magic fairy who picks up after everyone around the house? Well, I am the magic fairy!

        🐝 JULIA BERTRAND

*I*t's not uncommon for mothers to feel unappreciated. Much of what we do goes completely unnoticed. Others assume that the towels left on the floor magically disappear, or the peanut butter finds its way back into the cupboard. Isn't that the way it's always been?

The belief that "housework is women's work" is so deeply ingrained that even *we* take it for granted. As Arlie Hochschild points out in *Second Shift* "women worked roughly fifteen hours longer each week than men. Over a year, they worked an extra month of twenty-four-hour days a year." Is it any wonder why the majority of us feel like "slave labor"?

Until I realize that I can rewrite the "rules," I cannot make lasting changes in my home environment.

The past is a foreign country; they do things differently there.

✒ ANONYMOUS

*L*ooking back on our lives, it is difficult to imagine a time when we were not parents. The past is a "foreign country" where we used to live. How do we integrate the self that existed before motherhood with our new, emerging identity? How can we tend to the myriad changes going on inside of us when all our energy is consumed by a new infant? How can we maintain a sense of self?

For some mothers, the answer is journaling. "My journal, a longtime trusted companion, became a lifeline to my soul," writes Melinda Burns in *Mothering Magazine*. "It was a way of saying, 'You are here.'"

Some of us reflect on the past, remembering our hearts' yearnings and how we felt when we were alone. We make contact with our other selves, and feel who we are.

Connecting with my past integrates my various selves with who I am today.

*I never work better than when I am inspired by anger;
for when I am angry, I can write, pray, and preach
well, for then my whole temperament is quickened, my
understanding sharpened, and all mundane vexations
and temptations depart.*

☞ MARTIN LUTHER

nger is a powerful force. It can destroy and
it can create. It quickens the mind and
sharpens one's creativity. It obliterates distractions
and concentrates our focus. It feeds us.

When we do not transform our anger into fuel for
our creativity, it drains us. Instead of clearing our
vision, our anger clouds it. It weighs us down and
depresses us. We have cut ourself off from a vital
force within us. And in the process, we deprive our
children of both our energy and our love.

**When I deny my anger, it drains me. When I make
my anger mine, I can be released from its grip.**

What's done to children, they will do to society.
> KARL MENNINGER

I recently saw a disturbing documentary that reminded me how true Menninger's words are. The subject was abused children. A health care professional who ran a treatment center for troubled youth said that young children who have been abused and neglected are quite capable of cold-blooded murder because they are so detached from their feelings. They can't feel the results of their actions, therefore they have no conscience. "Their hearts need to heal," she said.

Society is not someone or something "out there." We are society. Our children mirror our hatred and bigotry, our prejudice and our violence—even if it's not directed at them. They are sirens that tell us when something is wrong with our society; they reflect our deep imbalances. That doesn't mean we need to be perfect parents, but we do need to be aware of the monumental effect we have on our children. After all, we create the society in which we want them to grow up.

Today, let me renew my commitment to my children and to society. They are one and the same.

Anyone who eats three meals a day should understand why cookbooks outsell sex books three to one.

⚓ L. M. BOYD

I was talking to a group of women during "mothers' night out." Inevitably, the topic of sex came up. One woman's husband kept complaining about their sex life. He felt it wasn't normal. He was sure that every other couple had resumed their conjugal relations fairly soon after their child's birth. To substantiate his claims, he telephoned his friends all over the country, asking them how often they were making love with their wives. Then, he announced his findings to his wife. "All my friends say they have sex once a week." In unison, the entire group of mothers cried, "they're lying!" That was all the proof I needed.

Working women do it less. Working mothers do it even lesser.

Selfness is an essential fact of life. The thought of nonselfness, precise sameness, is terrifying.

  LEWIS THOMAS

t is not uncommon for full-time homemakers to feel that our lives have become stagnant. We make valuable contributions to the life of our family, yet our individual pursuits get lost in the shuffle.

It's a fallacy to think that all our needs can be met by our family. Often we need to reach outside the home and family circle to find projects, activities, and relationships which enrich us. We need challenges that stretch us and encourage us to use our capacities to the fullest. By expanding our borders, we can maintain a sense of self which is separate and distinct from our role in the family.

I want to share myself with my family. To do that better, I must have my own endeavors so that there is more of myself to share.

*Before I married, I had six theories about bringing
up children, but no children; now I have six children
and no theories.*

❧ ANONYMOUS

*I*sn't it annoying when another mother who has
never been in our situation gives us advice
when we haven't asked for it? We feel invaded, out-
raged. We can't believe anyone would be so arrogant.
Then, one day, we catch ourselves giving the same
kind of "theoretical" advice when we haven't been
asked. That's when we get a quick lesson in humility.

Whenever we think we know what is best for
another mother, we're in trouble, especially when we
have never been in her shoes. We're assuming we can
make a better choice than she can make for herself,
and that's about as arrogant as one can get.

**Realizing I sound like all the "know-it-alls" I can't
stand is a humbling experience.**

Worrying helps you some. It seems as if you are doing something when you're worrying.

                   ❧ LUCY MAUD MONTGOMERY

*F*or some of us, worrying is a way to feel involved in our children's lives. By worrying, we illustrate our love and concern, but this isn't the best way to do it.

Children sense our moods. When we worry about them, we subtly communicate that they are not safe in the world. Our lack of trust inhibits their exploration and self-discovery. Our worries become their worries and, because they are not yet mature enough to separate real concerns from exaggerated ones, they become timid and reticent. They learn to fear the unknown and they feel anxious about the future.

Sure, we are all concerned with the well-being of our children. We want to protect them. But we can not prevent them from making their own mistakes. If we give them our trust as they venture out on their own, then they will trust themselves more and become more capable. Then we won't have to worry about them so much!

When I trust myself, I trust my children, and I worry less. Isn't this a better way to be involved in their lives?

Living In The Moment

I eagerly counted each of my first child's milestones. With my second, all I want to do is hold him like a baby.

🍼 AMY D'AGROSA

*T*here's something about having a first baby that turns mothers into record-keeping fanatics. We record every skill our infant masters as if he himself had invented it: Baby rolled over, discovered hands, laughed, sucked on toes. And we eagerly await each new accomplishment.

Sometimes we become so involved with our child's milestones that we forget to value the little things. We want our child to get to the next step; we want our child to grow up. We hear ourselves saying, "I hope he walks before his first birthday." We are in such a rush that we forget to cherish the fullness of every moment. And before we know it, our little one is not a baby anymore. They grow so fast....

When I try to speed up time, I rob myself of the richness of each moment.

There's a time when you have to explain to your children why they're born, and it's a marvelous thing if you know the reason by then.

HAZEL SCOTT

*D*uring the course of our children's early years, we will probably ask ourselves, "Why did I have this child?" Our answers will differ, depending on our mood and predicament. Eventually, as the months pass and turn into years, the primary reason emerges.

Although it's easy to forget why we originally decided to have children when we are buried in diapers and a perpetually messy house, we do know. And it's a marvelous thing that usually has nothing to do with the practicalities of life.

My children contribute to my life in a way no one else can. Let me be thankful for the richness they bring me.

For years, my husband and I have advocated separate vacations. But the kids keep finding us.

✑ Erma Bombeck

*E*ver notice that before we had children, we fantasized about going places with them, then we have children, and we fantasize about leaving them?

Every couple needs time alone and away from their children. Since kids are such a constant in our lives, it is easy to feel bound by them. Yet, each time we plan a trip, it seems some unforeseen emergency arises and we end up staying home. We lose money on non-refundable airline tickets, and we lose our patience.

Perhaps another approach might be more effective. Ever tried running away from home?

As Kahlil Gabran said of marriage: "Let there be spaces in your togetherness." This also applies to children.

There is no greater delight than to be conscious of sincerity on self-examination.

☞ MENCIUS

*E*veryone can tell us that we're "a great mother." But, ultimately, the real answer can only come from inside of us.

If we feel comfortable enough with who we are, both in our capabilities and shortcomings, there is no need to delude ourselves. To be sincere on self-examination, we need to transcend the harsh voices of criticism and feel self-compassion. We need to love ourselves and accept our inner beauty. Only then will we know if we're a "good mother."

**Self-examination is the search for inner truth.
If I am to be truthful in my search, I must love
what I am seeking.**

The third baby is the easiest one to have... You know, for instance, how you're going to look in a maternity dress about the seventh month, and you know how to release the footbrake on a baby carriage without fumbling amateurishly, and you know how to tie your shoes before and do knee-chests after, and while you're not exactly casual, you're a little offhand about the whole thing.

SHIRLEY JACKSON

here's nothing like experience!

By the time the third child comes along, we consider ourselves pros. We know what to expect during the delivery. We know the basic infant routine. We've experienced the full spectrum of childhood diseases, and we have a few tricks up our sleeves when things get rough.

No one mistakes us for a first-time mother because we don't look like the new mothers who are "fumbling amateurishly" with diapers and baby equipment. We have confidence. In fact, we're even a bit smug about the whole thing now that others come to us for advice. But not too smug: we remember when it was the other way around.

Motherhood never gets old, just more comfortable.

Babies are such a nice way to start people.

　 DON HEROLD

*B*abies *are* a nice way to start people. They're cuddly and soft, innocent and wide-eyed. But mothers, beware: babies grow into emotionally immature toddlers. Although they enjoy each other's company, demonstrating their affection with hugs and caresses, their mutual warmth quickly disappears whenever they want the same toy. In seconds, a perfectly good friendship is jeopardized by a ball or a yo-yo. Hitting, screaming, crying: these are the ways toddlers handle conflict. Negotiating a settlement between toddlers' disputes is left to the adults.

A father of a two-and-a-half-year-old once told me: "People who say things like 'Wouldn't the world be a better place if we were all more like children,' obviously don't have any kids of their own. If they did, they'd know that World War III would break out over a tinker toy!"

Being a baby is a good beginning, and it is only a beginning. Maturity comes with age.

*The mother-child relationship is paradoxical and,
in a sense, tragic. It requires the most intense love on
the mother's side, yet this very love must help the
child grow away from the mother and to become fully
independent.*

☛ ERICH FROMM

*L*earning how to let go is one of the biggest
challenges of motherhood. No matter how
intensely we think we want our child to be independent and self-sufficient, it is difficult and painful to
realize that we may not intercede on her behalf.

From day one, we discover that there are limits to
what we can do for our infant. When she wails, we
can only offer our soothing touch, we cannot remove
the shock of the outside world on her little system.
When she is struggling to focus her eyes or to lift her
tiny head, we can help. Yet, ultimately, it is only she
who can gain mastery of her body.

Painfully, we learn that the love we extend to help
her is the same love that gives her the strength to
grow away from and leave us. Our love is a worthy
paradox.

**"Letting go" is one way to demonstrate my love. It
shows my child that I trust her to trust herself.**

*There is an amazed curiosity in every young mother.
It is strangely miraculous to see and to hold a living
being formed within oneself and issued forth from
oneself.*

✎ SIMONE DE BEAUVOIR

*F*rom the moment our baby is born, we stare,
not quite believing the miracle that has issued
forth from our bodies. Our minds still can't quite
fathom the mystery of the birth experience.

When asleep, we peek in her room and again, we
stare, studying her face for the answer to our question: "Is she real?" Enchanted, we continue to gaze at
her, amazed that she has come into our lives.

Our curiosity never completely goes away. Over
the years, there are certain moments when we find
ourselves simply gazing at our child and once more
ask: "Did this person really come from inside of me?"

**The miraculous qualities of birth never leave me.
Maybe that's what makes it so special.**

Grateful acknowledgement is given for permission to reprint the following:

Quotes from Mary Shelley, Sojourner Truth, Jean Stafford, Joanna Field, Ivy Baker Priest, and Ilka Chase from *The Quotable Woman From Eve To 1799.* Copyright © 1982 by Elaine Partnow. Reprinted by permission of Facts On File, Inc., New York. And, *The Quotable Woman: 1800–1981.*

Karin Boye, "Yes It Hurts," translated from Swedish by May Swenson in *Half Sun Half Sleep,* by Charles Scribner's Sons. Coypright © 1967 by May Swenson. Reprinted by permission of May Swenson's Estate.

John Crowe Ransom, "Bells for John Whiteside's Daughter" copyright © 1924 by Alfred A. Knopf, renewed 1952 by John Crowe Ransom. Reprinted by permission of Random House, Inc.

Confucius, "The Book of Songs," *The Wisdom of Confucius,* ed. Lin Yutang. Copyright © 1938, renewed 1966 by Random House, Inc. Reprinted by permission of the publisher.

W.H. Auden, "In Memory of W.B. Yeats," *The Collected Poetry of W.H. Auden.* Copyright © 1945 by W.H. Auden. Reprinted by permission of Random House, Inc.

Allende, Isabel. *Eva Luna.* New York: Alfred A. Knopf, Inc., 1988.

Barry, Dave. *Babies and Other Hazards of Sex.* Emmaus, Pennsylvania: Rodale Press, 1984.

Bartlett, John. *Bartlett's Familiar Quotations.* Boston: Little, Brown and Company, 1980.

Bloomsbury Thematic Dictionary of Quotations. London: Bloomsbury Publishing, Ltd., 1988.

Burns, Melinda. "Reclaiming the Mother Within." *Mothering Magazine* (Summer 1991), p. 41

Byrne, Robert, ed. *1,911 Best Things Anybody Ever Said.* New York: Fawcett Columbine (Ballantine Books), 1988.

Cohen, J.M., and Cohen, M.J., eds. *The Penguin Dictionary of Modern Quotations.* London: Penguin Books, Ltd., 1980.

Fitzhenry, Robert I., ed. *Barnes and Noble Book of Quotations.* New York: Barnes and Noble (Harper and Row Publishers, Inc.), 1986.

Friedland, Ronnie, and Kort, Carol, eds. *A Mother's Journal: A Keepsake Book for Thoughts and Dreams.* Philadelphia: Running Press, 1985.

Galland, China. *Longing for Darkness*. New York: Viking Penguin, 1991.

Galyean, Dorothy. *Quips, Quotes & Cleaned Up Jokes #1*. 1988.

_____. *Quips, Quotes & Cleaned Up Jokes #2*. 1988.

Gardner, John, and Reese, Francesca Gardner. *Know or Listen to Those Who Know: A Book of Quotations*. New York: W.W. Norton and Co., 1975.

George, Leslie. "The Loneliness of Motherhood." *American Health* (March 1989), p. 114.

Genevie, Louis E., and Margolies, Eva. *The Motherhood Report / How Women Feel About Being Mothers*. New York: Macmillan, 1987.

Hart, Louise. "Self-Esteem: The Best Gift You Can Give Your Child—And Yourself." *Mothering Magazine* (Spring 1989), p. 95.

Hochschild, Arlie. *The Second Shift*. New York: Avon Books (The Hearst Corporation), 1989.

James, Sally. "Too Precious Parenting." *Mothering Magazine* (Summer 1990), p. 25.

Lamb, G.F., ed. *Apt and Amusing Quotations*. Kingswood, U.K.: Paperfronts Elliot Right Way Books, 1986.

Leach, Penelope. *Your Baby and Child from Birth to Age Five.* New York: Alfred A. Knopf, 1978.

Lindbergh, Anne Morrow. *Gift from the Sea.* New York: Vintage Books (Random House), 1955.

Mason, Jerry, ed. *The Family of Woman.* New York: Perigee Books (Putnam Publishing Group), 1979.

Nagashima, Yoshiaki. *One World, One People.* Tokyo: ARC International, 1984.

Noble, Vicki. *Motherpeace: A Way to the Goddess Through Myth, Art, and Tarot.* New York: Harper and Row Publishers, Inc., 1983.

O'Mara, Peggy. "Like A Weaning." *Mothering Magazine* (Spring 1991), p. 2.

Partnow, Elaine, ed. *The Quotable Woman from Eve to 1799.* New York: Facts on File, 1985.

———. *The Quotable Woman: 1800-1981.* New York: Facts on File, 1982.

Pepper, Frank S., ed. *The Wit and Wisdom of the 20th Century: A Dictionary of Quotations.* New York: Bedrick Books, 1987.

Peter, Dr. Laurence J. *Peter's Quotations, Ideas for Our Time.* New York: William Morrow and Company, 1977.

The Quotable Woman. Philadelphia: Running Press, 1991.

Simpson, James B., ed., *Simpson's Contemporary Quotations.* New York: Houghton Mifflin, 1988.

Steele, Della White. "Home Mommy." *Mothering Magazine* (Spring 1987), p. 98.

Steichen, Edward. *The Family of Man.* New York: The Museum of Modern Art, 1955.

Towle, Alexandra, ed. *Mothers: A Celebration in Prose, Poetry, and Photographs of Mothers and Motherhood.* New York: Simon and Schuster, 1988

Tripp, Rhoda Thomas, ed. *The International Thesaurus of Quotations.* New York: Perennial Library (Harper and Row, Publishers, Inc.), 1970.

White, Janet McCormick. "Downwardly Mobile." *Mothering Magazine* (Spring 1990), p. 93.

Winokur, John, ed. *Friendly Advice.* New York: Dutton (Penguin Group), 1990.